The Economist

STYLE GUIDE

The
Economist
Books

BUSINESS BOOKS

First published 1986 by The Economist Publications Ltd as
The Economist Pocket Style Book

This completely revised, expanded and reset edition first
published in Great Britain by Business Books Limited,
an imprint of Random Century Limited, Random Century
House, 20 Vauxhall Bridge Road, London SW1V 2SA,
in association with The Economist Books Ltd.

Editor Penny Butler
Illustrations by Rufus Segar
Sub-editors Isla MacLean, Michelle Clark
Editorial Assistants Eleanor Martlew, Sara Harper,
Jeremy Haworth
Editorial Director Stephen Brough
Art Director Douglas Wilson
Production Assistant Christine Campbell

Any correspondence regarding this publication should be
addressed to: The Editorial Director, The Economist Books,
Axe and Bottle Court, 70 Newcomen Street, London
SE1 1YT

A catalogue record for this book is available from The
British Library

ISBN 0 09-174616-7

Printed in Great Britain by Butler and Tanner,
Frome, Somerset

CONTENTS

PREFACE

Every newspaper has its own style book, a set of rules telling journalists whether to write **Peking** or **Beijing**, **Gadaffi** or **Qaddafi**, **judgement** or **judgment**. *The Economist*'s style book does this and a bit more. It also warns writers of some common mistakes, and encourages them to write with more clarity and simplicity. This edition of the style book is largely the work of John Grimond, the foreign editor.

To make the style guide of wider general interest, additional material has been added, drawing on the series of reference books published under The Economist Books imprint.

All the prescriptive judgments in this style guide, however, are directly derived from those used each week in writing and editing *The Economist*.

Throughout the text, bold type is used to indicate examples. Words in SMALL CAPITALS indicate a separate but relevant entry (except in the paragraphs headed ABBREVIATIONS, where the use of small capitals is discussed).

This new updated and expanded edition of *The Economist Style Guide* has been reorganised into three sections. The first is based on the style book used by those who edit *The Economist*. The second, on American and British English, describes the main differences between the two great English-speaking areas, in spelling, grammar and usage. The third part gathers together in one place all the reference material, and includes some new entries.

INTRODUCTION

On only two scores can *The Economist* hope to outdo its rivals consistently. One is the quality of its analysis; the other is the quality of its writing. The aim of this style guide is to give general advice on writing, to point out some common errors and to set some arbitrary rules. The first requirement of *The Economist* is that it should be readily understandable. Clarity of writing usually follows clarity of thought. So think what you want to say, then say it as simply as possible. Keep in mind George Orwell's six elementary rules ("Politics and the English Language", 1946):

1. Never use a METAPHOR, simile or other figure of speech which you are used to seeing in print.
2. Never use a long word where a SHORT WORD will do.
3. If it is possible to cut out a word, always cut it out.
4. Never use the passive where you can use the ACTIVE.
5. Never use a FOREIGN PHRASE, a scientific word or a JARGON word if you can think of an everyday English equivalent.
6. Break any of these rules sooner than say anything outright barbarous.

The reader is primarily interested in what you have to say. By the way in which you say it you may encourage him either to read on or to stop reading. If you want him to read on:

1. Do not be stuffy. "To write a genuine, familiar or truly English style", said Hazlitt, "is to write as anyone would speak in common conversation who had a thorough command or choice of words or who could discourse with ease, force and perspicuity setting aside all pedantic and oratorical flourishes."

Use the language of everyday speech, not that of spokesmen, lawyers or bureaucrats (so prefer **let** to **permit, people** to **persons, buy** to **purchase, colleague** to **peer, way out** to **exit, present** to **gift, rich** to **wealthy, break** to **violate**). Only property developers and tongue-tied ambassadors talk about refurbishment. **Refurbishment of The Economist Building complex** means **doing up The Economist Building and its neighbours.**

Avoid, where possible, euphemisms and circumlocutions promoted by interest-groups. The **hearing-impaired** are simply **deaf.** It is no disrespect to the **disabled** sometimes to describe them as **crippled. Female teenagers** are **girls,** not **women.** The **under-**

privileged may be **disadvantaged,** but are more likely just **poor.**

And **man** sometimes includes **woman,** just as **he** sometimes makes do for **she** as well. So long as you are not insensitive in other ways, few women will be offended if you do not use **or she** after every **he.**

> He or she which hath no stomach to this fight,
> Let him or her depart; his or her passport shall be made,
> And crowns for convoy put into his or her purse:
> We would not die in that person's company
> That fears his or her fellowship to die with us.

2. Do not be hectoring or arrogant. Those who disagree with you are not necessarily stupid or insane. Nobody needs to be described as silly: let your analysis prove that he is.

3. Do not be too pleased with yourself. Don't boast of your own cleverness by telling readers that you correctly predicted something or that you have a scoop. You are more likely to bore or irritate them than to impress them. So keep references to *The Economist* to a minimum, particularly those of the we-told-you-so variety. References to "this correspondent" or "your correspondent" are always self-conscious and often self-congratulatory.

4. Do not be too chatty. **Surprise, surprise** is more irritating than informative. So is **Ho, ho,** etc.

5. Do not be too didactic. A recent issue of *The Economist* had an imperative on six out of seven consecutive pages. If too many sentences begin **Compare, Consider, Expect, Imagine, Look at, Note, Prepare for, Remember** or **Take,** readers will think they are reading a textbook (or, indeed, a style book). This may not be the way to persuade them to renew their subscriptions.

6. Do not be sloppy in the construction of your sentences and paragraphs. Do not use a participle unless you make it clear what it applies to. Thus avoid **Having died, they had to bury him,** or **Proceeding along this line of thought, the cause of the train crash becomes clear.**

Don't overdo the use of **don't, isn't, can't, won't,** etc.

Use the subjunctive properly. If you are posing a hypothesis contrary to fact, you must use the subjunctive. Thus, **If Hitler were alive today, he could tell us whether he kept a diary.** If the hypothesis may or may not be true, you do not use the subjunctive: **If this diary is not Hitler's, we shall be glad we did not publish it.** If you have **would** in the main clause, you must use the subjunctive in the **if** clause. **If you were to disregard this rule, you would make a fool of yourself.**

Do your best to be lucid. Simple sentences help. Keep complicated constructions and gimmicks to a minimum, if necessary by remembering the *New Yorker*'s comment: "Backward ran sentences until reeled the mind." Mark Twain described how a good writer treats sentences: "At times he may indulge himself with a long one, but he will make sure there are no folds in it, no vaguenesses, no parenthetical interruptions of its view as a whole; when he has done with it, it won't be a sea-serpent with half of its arches under the water; it will be a torch-light procession."

Long paragraphs, like long sentences, can confuse the reader. "The paragraph," according to Fowler, "is essentially a unit of thought, not of length; it must be homogeneous in subject matter and sequential in treatment." One-sentence paragraphs should be used only occasionally.

Clear thinking is, in fact, the key to clear writing. "A scrupulous writer," observed Orwell, "in every sentence that he writes will ask himself at least four questions, thus: What am I trying to say? What words will express it? What image or idiom will make it clearer? Is this image fresh enough to have an effect? And he will probably ask himself two more: Could I put it more shortly? Have I said anything that is avoidably ugly?"

Scrupulous writers will also notice that their copy is edited only lightly and is likely to be used. It may even be read.

A NOTE ON EDITING

Editing has always made a large contribution to *The Economist*'s excellence. It should continue to do so. But editing on a screen is beguilingly simple. It is quite easy to rewrite an article without realising that one has done much to it at all: the cursor leaves no trace of crossings-out, handwritten insertions, rearranged sentences or reordered paragraphs. The temptation is to continue to make changes until something emerges which the editor himself might have written. One benefit of this is a tightly edited newspaper. One cost is a certain sameness. The risk is that the newspaper will turn into a collection of 70 or 80 articles which read as though they have been written by no more than half a dozen hands. *The Economist* has a single editorial outlook, and it is anonymous. But it is the work of many people, both in London and abroad, as its datelines testify. If the prose of our Tokyo correspondent is indistinguishable from the prose of our Nairobi correspondent, readers will feel they are being robbed of variety. They may also wonder whether these two people really exist, or whether the entire newspaper is not written in London. The moral for editors is that they should respect good writing. That is mainly what this style guide is designed to promote. It is not intended to impose a single style on all *The Economist*'s journalists. A writer's style, after all, should reflect his mind and personality. So long as they are compatible with *The Economist*'s, and so long as the prose is good, editors should exercise suitable self-restraint. Remember that your copy, too, will be edited. And even if you think you are not guilty, bear in mind this comment from John Gross:

> Most writers I know have tales to tell of being mangled by editors and mauled by fact-checkers, and naturally it is the flagrant instances they choose to single out – absurdities, outright distortions of meaning, glaring errors. But most of the damage done is a good deal less spectacular. It consists of small changes (usually too boring to describe to anyone else) that flatten a writer's style, slow down his argument, neutralise his irony; that ruin the rhythm of a sentence or the balance of a paragraph; that deaden the tone that makes the music. I sometimes think of the process as one of "de-sophistication".

John Grimond

PART I

THE ESSENCE OF STYLE

A

ABBREVIATIONS. Unless an abbreviation or acronym is so familiar that it is used more often than the full form (eg, **BBC**, **CIA**, **DNA**, **EC**, **FBI**, **GATT**, **IMF**, **NATO**, **OECD**), write the words in full on first appearance: thus **Trades Union Congress** (not **TUC**). After the first mention, try not to repeat the abbreviation too often; so write **the agency** rather than **the IAEA**, **the Community** rather than **the EC**, to avoid spattering the page with capital letters. There is no need to give the initials of an organisation if it is not referred to again.

If an abbreviation can be pronounced (eg, **EFTA**, **NATO**, **UNESCO**), it does not generally require the definite article. (**GATT**, however, is sometimes called **the GATT**.) Other organisations, except companies, should usually be preceded by **the** (**the BBC**, **the DSS**, **the KGB**, **the UNCHR** and **the NIESR**). Use **MP** only after first spelling out Member of Parliament in full (in many places an **MP** is a military policeman).

Abbreviations that can be pronounced and are composed of bits of words rather than just initials should be spelled out in upper and lower case: **Comecon, Frelimo, Legco, Renamo.** (See also INITIALS.)

In bodymatter, abbreviations, whether they can be pronounced as words or not (**GNP**, **GDP**, **FOB**, **CIF**, **A**-levels, **D**-marks, **T**-shirts, **X**-rays), should be set in small capitals, with no points – unless they are currencies like **DM** or **FFr**, or degrees of temperature like °F and °C. Brackets, apostrophes (see PUNCTUATION) and all other typographical furniture accompanying small capitals are generally set in ordinary roman, with a lower-case s (also roman) for plurals and genitives. Thus **IOUs**, **MPS'** salaries, (**SDRs**), etc. But ampersands are set as small capitals, as are numerals and any hyphens attaching them to a small capital. Thus **R&D**, **A23**, **M1**, **F-16**, etc. See also AMPERSANDS.

Abbreviations that include upper-case and lower-case letters must be set in a mixture of small capitals and lower case: **BAe, BPhil, PhDs**.

In headings, rubrics, cross-heads, flytitles, captions, tables, charts (including sources), use ordinary caps, not small caps.

Use lower case for **kg, km, lb** (never **lbs**), **mph** and other MEASURES, and for **ie, eg**, which should both be followed by commas. When used with figures, these lower-case abbreviations should follow immediately, with no space (**11am, 15kg, 35mm, 100mph, 78rpm**), as should **AD** and **BC** (**76AD, 55BC**), though they are set in small capitals. Two abbreviations together, however, must be separated: **60m b/d**.

Most scientific units, except those of temperature, that are named after individuals should be set in small capitals, though any attachments denoting multiples go in lower case. Thus **watt** is **w**, whereas **kilowatt, milliwatt** and **megawatt**, meaning **1,000 watts, one thousandth of a watt** and **1m watts**, are abbreviated to **kw, mw** and **MW**.

The elements do not take small capitals. **Lead** is **Pb, carbon dioxide** is CO_2, **methane** is CH_4. **Chlorofluorocarbons** are, however, **CFCs**, and the **oxides of nitrogen** are generally **NOX**. Different isotopes of the same element are distinguished by raised prefixes: **carbon-14** is ^{14}C, **helium-3** is ^3He.

Most upper-case abbreviations take upper-case initial letters when written in full (eg, the **LSO** is the **London Symphony Orchestra**), but there are exceptions: **CAP** but **common agricultural policy**, **EMU** but **economic and monetary union**, **GDP** but **gross domestic product**, **PSBR** but **public-sector borrowing requirement**, **VLSI** but **very large-scale integration**.

Do not use **Prof, Sen, Gen, Col**, etc. **Lieut-Colonel** and **Lieut-Commander** are permissible. So is **Rev**, but it must be preceded by **the** and followed by a Christian name or initial: **the Rev Jesse Jackson** (thereafter **Mr Jackson**).

Always spell out **page, pages, hectares, miles**. But **kilograms** (not **kilogrammes**) and **kilometres** can be shortened to **kg** (or **kilos**) and **km**.

Remember that **EFTA** is the **European Free Trade Association**, the **FAO** is the **Food and Agriculture Organisation**, the **IDA** is the **International Development Association**, the **OAU** is the **Organisation of African Unity**, the **PLO** is the **Palestine Liberation Organisation**.

Write **Euro-MPs**, not **MEPs**.

-ABLE, -EABLE, -IBLE. The following lists are not comprehensive.

-able

analysable
bribable
debatable
dispensable
disputable
forgivable
imaginable

implacable
indescribable
indictable
indistinguishable
manoeuvrable
ratable

salable (*but prefer* sellable)
tradable
unmistakable
unshakable
usable

-eable

bridgeable
manageable

peaceable
serviceable

sizeable
traceable

11

-ible

accessible	defensible	legible
admissible	destructible	negligible
audible	digestible	ostensible
collapsible	eligible	perceptible
combustible	feasible	permissible
compatible	inadmissible	repressible
comprehensible	indestructible	reproducible
convertible	investible	submersible
corruptible	irascible	tangible

ACCENTS. On words now accepted as English, use accents only when they make a crucial difference to pronunciation: **cliché, soupçon, façade, café, communiqué**. If you use one accent, use all: **émigré, mêlée, protégé, résumé**. See also ACCENTS, page 89.

Put the accents and cedillas on French names and words, and umlauts on German ones: **François Mitterrand, Karl Otto Pöhl**. In other foreign languages, either use all the accents on proper nouns (names, places, etc) correctly or none.

Any foreign word in italics should, however, be given its proper accents.

ACTIVE, NOT PASSIVE. It is not incumbent upon you to be pompous.

ADVERBS. Put adverbs where you would put them in normal speech. See also AMERICANISMS, page 13 and PART II.

AFFECT means **to have an influence on**, as in **The novel affected his attitude to immigrants**. See also EFFECT.

AFFINITY is by definition mutual. It can exist **between** or **with** things, but not **to** or **for** them.

AGGRAVATE means **make worse**, not **irritate** or **annoy**.

AGGRESSION is an unattractive quality, so do not call a **keen** salesman an aggressive one (unless his foot is in the door – or beyond).

AGONY COLUMN: when Sherlock Holmes perused this, it was a **personal column**, not letters to an **agony aunt**.

AGREE: things are agreed **on**, **to** or **about**, not just agreed.

ALIBI: an **alibi** is the proven fact of being elsewhere, not a false explanation.

ALTERNATE, as an adjective, means **every other**.

ALTERNATIVE: strictly, this is **one of two**, not one of three, four, five or more (which may be **options**).

AMEND is not quite the same as **emend**; though both result in an improvement, **emend** is used only of something written. **He amended his life by giving up gambling and drinking,** but **He emended his memo by correcting the spelling mistakes.**

AMERICANISMS. Use Americanisms discriminatingly. Many American words and expressions have passed into the language; others have vigour, particularly if used occasionally. Some are short and to the point (so prefer **lay off** to **make redundant**). But many are unnecessarily long (so use **and** not **additionally, car** not **automobile, company** not **corporation, transport** not **transportation, district** not **neighbourhood, oblige** not **obligate, stocks** not **inventories** unless there is the risk of confusion with stocks and shares).

Choose tenses according to British usage. In particular, do not fight shy of the perfect tense, especially where no date or time is given. Thus **Mr Bush has woken up to the danger** is preferable to **Mr Bush woke up to the danger,** unless you can add **last week** or **when he heard the explosion.**

Americans put the adverbs before the verb; the British put them after, as in normal speech. See also PART II.

AMPERSANDS. Ampersands should be used as follows.
1. When they are part of the name of a company (eg, AT&T, **Pratt & Whitney**).
2. For such things as constituencies where two names are linked to form one unit (eg, **The rest of Brighouse & Spenborough joined with the Batley part of Batley & Morley to form Batley & Spen. Or The area thus became the Pakistani province of Kashmir and the Indian state of Jammu & Kashmir**).
3. In R&D, S&L.

AN should be used before a word beginning with a vowel or an h if, and only if, the h is silent. So **a hospital, a hotel**, but **an honorary degree**.

ANIMALS, PLANTS, ETC. When it is necessary to use a Latin name, follow the standard practice. Thus for all creatures higher than viruses, write the binomial name in italics, giving an initial capital to the first word (the genus): **Turdus turdus**, the song thrush; **Metasequoia glyptostroboides**, the dawn redwood.

ANTICIPATE does not mean **expect**. Jack and Jill expected to marry; if they anticipated marriage, only Jill might find herself expectant.

ANY ONE refers to a number; **anyone** to anybody.

ANY WAY refers to any manner; **anyway** means **nevertheless**.

APPEAL is intransitive nowadays (except in America), so **appeal against** decisions.

APPRAISE means **set a price on. Apprise** means **inform**.

AS OF (April 5th or April): prefer **on** (or **after**, or **since**) April 5th, in April.

AS TO: there is usually a more appropriate preposition.

AUTARCHY means **absolute sovereignty** but **autarky** means **self-sufficiency**.

B

BALE: in the hayfield, yes, otherwise **bail, bail out.**

BEG THE QUESTION means neither **invite the question** nor **evade the answer.** To **beg the question** is to base a conclusion upon an assumption that is as much in need of proof as the conclusion itself.

BIANNUAL can mean **twice a year** or **once every two years.** Avoid.

BICENTENNIAL: prefer **bicentenary** (as a noun).

BLACK: in the black means **in profit** in Britain, but **making losses** in some places. Always use **in profit.**

BOTH ... AND: a preposition placed after **both** should be repeated after **and.** Thus, **both to right and to left;** but **to both right and left** is all right.

Apply the same rule to **either ... or ... , neither ... nor ...** and **not only ... but (also) ...**

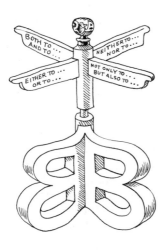

C

CANUTE'S exercise on the seashore was designed to persuade his courtiers of what he knew to be true but they doubted, ie, that he was not omnipotent. Don't imply he was surprised to get his feet wet.

CAPITALS.
A balance has to be struck between so many capitals that the eyes dance and so few that the reader is diverted more by our style than by our substance. The general rule is to dignify with capital letters organisations and institutions, but not people. More exact rules are laid out below. Even these, however, leave some decisions to individual judgment. If in doubt use lower case unless it looks absurd. And remember that "a foolish consistency is the hobgoblin of little minds" (Emerson).

1. People. Use upper case for ranks and titles when written in conjunction with a name, but lower case when on their own. Thus, **President Bush,** but the **president**; **Vice-President Quayle,** but the **vice-president**; **Colonel Qaddafi** but the **colonel**; **Pope John Paul,** but the **pope**; **Queen Elizabeth,** but the **queen.**

Do not write **Prime Minister Major** or **Defence Secretary Cheney**; they are the **prime minister, Mr Major,** and the **defence secretary, Mr Cheney.** You may, however, write **Chancellor Kohl.**

All office holders when referred to merely by their office, not by their name, are lower case: the **chancellor of the exchequer,** the **foreign secretary,** the **prime minister,** the **speaker,** the **treasury secretary,** the **president of the United States,** the **chairman of British Coal.**

The only exceptions are: (a) a few titles that would look unduly peculiar without capitals, eg, **Black Rod, Master of the Rolls, Chancellor of the Duchy of Lancaster, Lord Privy Seal, Lord Chancellor**; (b) a few exalted people, such as the **Dalai Lama,** the **Aga Khan.** Also **God.** See also TITLES.

2. Organisations, ministries, departments, treaties, acts, etc, generally take upper case when their full name (or something pretty close to it, eg, **State Department**) is used. Thus, **European Commission, Forestry Commission, Arab League, Amnesty International,** the **Household Cavalry, Ministry of Agriculture, Department of Trade and Industry, Treasury, Metropolitan Police, High Court, Supreme Court, Court of Appeal, Senate,**

Central Committee, Politburo, Oxford University, the **New York Stock Exchange** (but the **London stock exchange**, since that is only its informal name), the **Treaty of Rome**, the **Health and Safety at Work Act**, etc.

So, too, the **House of Commons, House of Lords, House of Representatives, St Paul's Cathedral** (the **cathedral**), **World Bank** (the **Bank**), **Bank of England** (the **Bank**), **Department of State** (the **department**).

But organisations, committees, commissions, special groups, etc, that are either impermanent, ad hoc, local or relatively insignificant should be lower case. Thus: the **subcommittee on journalists' rights of the National Executive Committee of the Labour Party**, the **international economic subcommittee of the Senate Foreign Relations Committee**, the **Oxford University bowls club, Market Blandings rural district council**.

Use lower case for rough descriptions (the **safety act**, the **American health department**, the **French parliament**, as distinct from its **National Assembly**). If you are not sure whether the English translation of a foreign name is exact or not, assume it is rough and use lower case.

Parliament and **Congress** are upper case. But the **opposition** is lower case, even when used in the sense of **her majesty's loyal opposition**. The **government**, the **administration** and the **cabinet** are always lower case.

3. The full name of political parties is upper case, including the word party: **Republican Party, Labour Party, Peasants' Party**. Note that only people are **Democrats, Christian Democrats, Liberal Democrats** or **Social Democrats**; their parties, policies, committees, etc, are **Democratic, Christian Democratic, Liberal Democratic** or **Social Democratic** (although a committee may be **Democrat-controlled**).

When referring to a specific party, write **Labour**, the **Republican nominee**, a prominent **Liberal**, etc, but use lower case in looser references to **liberals, conservatism, communists**, etc. **Tories**, however, are upper case.

4. A political, economic or religious label formed from a proper name, eg, **Gaullism, Paisleyite, Leninist, Napoleonic, Jacobite, Luddite, Marxist, Hobbesian, Christian, Buddhism, Hindu, Maronite, Finlandisation, Thatcherism**, should have a capital.

5. In finance and government there are some particular exceptions to the general rule of initial caps for full names, lower case for informal ones. Use caps for the **World Bank** and the **Fed** (after first spelling it out as the **Federal Reserve**), although these are shortened, informal names. The **Bank of England** and its foreign equiva-

lents have initial caps when named formally and separately, but collectively they are central banks in lower case (except Ireland's, which is actually named the **Central Bank**). **Special drawing rights** are lower case but abbreviated in small caps as **SDR**s, except when used with a figure as a currency (**SDR500m**). **Deutschemarks** are D-**marks**. Treasury bonds issued by America's Treasury should be upper case; treasury bills (or bonds) of a general kind should be lower case. Avoid **T-bonds** and **t-bills**.

After first mention, the **House of Commons** (or **Lords**, or **Representatives**) becomes the **House**, the **World Bank** and **Bank of England** become the **Bank** and the **IMF** can become the **Fund**. Organisations with unusual names, such as the **African National Congress**, **Civic Forum** and the **European Community**, become the **Congress**, the **Forum** and the **Community**. But most other organisations – agencies, banks, commissions (including the **European Commission**), etc – take lower case when referred to incompletely on second mention.

6. Places. Use initial capitals for definite geographical places, regions, areas and countries (**The Hague, Transylvania, Germany**), and for vague but recognised political or geographical areas: the **Middle East, South Atlantic, East Asia** (which is to be preferred to the **Far East**), the **West** (as in the decline of the West), the **Gulf, North Atlantic, South-East Asia**, the **Midlands, Central America**, the **West Country, Western Europe**.

Use lower case for **east, west, north, south** except when part of a name (**North Korea, South Africa, West End**) or when part of a thinking group: the **South** (in the United States), the **Highlands** (of Scotland). But use lower case if you are, say, comparing regions of the United States, some of which are merely geographical areas: **House prices in the north-east and the south are rising faster than those in the mid-west and the south-west**.

Use **West Germany (Berlin)** and **East Germany (Berlin)** only in historical references. They are now **western Germany (Berlin)** and **eastern Germany**.

The **third world** (an unsatisfactory term now that the communist second world has all but disappeared) is lower case.

If in doubt, use lower case (**the sunbelt**).

Use capitals for particular buildings, even if the name is not strictly accurate (eg, the **Foreign Office**).

Lower case for province, county, state, city when not strictly part of the name: **Washington state, Cabanas province, Guatemala city, Kuwait city, New York city, Panama city, Quebec city** (but **Dodge City, Ho Chi Minh City, Kansas City, Oklahoma City, Quezon City, Salt Lake City**).

7. Others

Some political terms (upper case)

Communist (if a particular party) Congress
the Crown   Tory
Parliament   the Twelve
Teamster   Warsaw Pact

Historical periods (upper case)

Black Death   Renaissance
the Depression   Restoration
Middle Ages   Year of the Dog (but new year
New Deal   and new year's day)
Reconstruction

Trade names (upper case)

Hoover, Teflon, Valium, etc

Miscellaneous (upper case)

anti-Semitism   Mafia (the genuine article)
the Bar   Pershing missile (because it is
Catholics   named after somebody)
Coloureds (in South Africa)   Protestants
the Cup Final   Pyrrhic
the Davis Cup   Sandinist (*not* Sandinista)
Eurobond   Semitic (-ism)
Euroyen bond   Test match
Hispanics   Utopia (-n)
House of Laity   Young Turks

Miscellaneous (lower case)

19th amendment   the left
  (*but* Article 19)   mafia (any old group
aborigines   of criminals)
administration   new year
blacks   new year's day
cabinet   opposition
civil servant   the pope
civil service   the press
common market   the queen
communist (generally)   the right
constitution   the shah
cruise missile   the speaker
cultural revolution   third world
french windows   "state of the union" message
general synod   white paper
government

CASE: "There is perhaps no single word so freely resorted to as a trouble-saver," says Gowers, "and consequently responsible for so much flabby writing." Often you can do without it. **There are many cases of it being unnecessary** is better as **It is often unnecessary. If it is the case that** ... simply means **If. It is not the case** means **It is not so.**

CASSANDRA's predictions were correct but not believed.

CATALYST: this is something that speeds up a chemical reaction while itself remaining unchanged. Do not confuse it with one of the agents.

CENSOR. The critics may **censure** a bad play, but oppose any attempt to **censor** it, that is **suppress all or part** of it.

CENTRED on, not **around** or **in**.

CHARGE: if you **charge** intransitively, do so as a bull, cavalry officer or some such, not as an **accuser** (so avoid **The standard of writing was abysmal, he charged**).

CIRCUMSTANCES stand **around** a thing, so it is **in**, not **under**, them.

CLICHES. As H.W. and F.G. Fowler point out, "Hackneyed phrases become hackneyed because they are useful in the first instance; but they derive a new efficiency from the very fact that they are hackneyed." Use a familiar phrase if it expresses your meaning clearly, but not simply because it is familiar.

COIFFED, not **coiffured**.

COLLAPSE is not transitive. You may collapse, but you may not collapse something.

COLLECTIVE NOUNS. There is no firm rule about the number of a verb governed by a singular collective noun. It is best to go by the sense, ie, whether the collective noun stands for a single entity (**The council was elected in March, The army is on a voluntary basis**) or for its constituents (**The council are at sixes and sevens over rates, The army are above the average civilian height**).
A safe rule for **number: The number is ... , A number are ...**
A **pair** and a **couple** are both plural.
A **government**, a **party**, a **company** (whether Tesco or Marks and Spencer) and a **partnership** (Skidmore, Owings & Merrill) are all **it**, and take a singular verb. So does a **country**, even if its name looks plural. Thus **The United States is helping the Philippines.**

The **United Nations** is singular.

Brokers too. **Citicorp Scrimgeour Vickers is preparing a statement.** Avoid **stockbrokers Citicorp Scrimgeour Vickers, bankers Chase Manhattan** or **accountants Peat Marwick McClintock.** And remember that **Barclays is a British bank,** not the British bank, just as **Ford is a car company,** not the car company and **Luciano Pavarotti is an opera singer,** not the opera singer.

Some nouns ending in **s** are always treated as singular; they include **news** and games such as **darts, bowls** and **billiards.**

COME UP WITH: try **suggest, originate** or **produce.**

COMPANIES.
Call companies by the names they call themselves. Here are some confusing ones.

Airbus Industrie
Aérospatiale
Allied-Lyons
American Telephone and
  Telegraph (AT&T)
Anglo American
B.A.T Industries
Banc One
Bank of America
Bayerische Hypotheken- und
  Wechsel-Bank (space before
  the und, no hyphen after)
Bloomingdale's
Boots (the chemist)
British Aerospace (BAe)
W.I. Carr (sometimes known
  as WICO)
CASA (Spanish Airbus partner;
  not Construcciones
  Aeronauticas SA in full)
Chesebrough-Pond's
Coca-Cola
Consolidated Gold Fields
  (abbreviated to ConsGold)
County NatWest
Cummins Engine
de Havilland
Donaldson, Lufkin & Jenrette
Du Pont
Eastern Air Lines

Ernst & Young
Fried. Krupp
Gimbels
Goldman Sachs
Hamleys
Hanson (*not* Trust), Hanson
  Industries (the American arm)
Harrods
Hoare Govett
Hongkong and Shanghai Bank
Japan Air Lines
Kohlberg Kravis Roberts
Lloyd's (insurance market)
Lloyds Bank
Lord & Taylor
McDonald's
McDonnell Douglas
Marks and Spencer (*but* Marks
  & Spencer is the name above
  the shop)
Marshall Field
Merrell
Merrill Lynch
Messerschmitt-Bölkow-Blohm
  (MBB)
Moët & Chandon
J.P. Morgan
Motoren Turbine Union
NeXT (Steve Jobs's computer
  firm, *not* Britain's retailer)

Nippon Telegraph and
  Telephone
Olympia & York
Pan Am
Pillsbury
Pratt & Whitney
Procter & Gamble
Ranks Hovis McDougall
Rich's
Rolls-Royce (cars and
  aero engines)
Saks Fifth Avenue
Salomon Brothers
savings and loan associations
  (*not* loans)
Sears, Roebuck & Co.
Securities and Investments
  Board

Shearson Lehman Hutton
Short Brothers
W.H. Smith, *but* WH Smith is
  the name above the shop
SmithKline Beecham or
  SmithKline
Smith New Court
Standard & Poor's
Time Warner
Tonen Corporation (formerly
  Toa Nenryo)
Toys " Я " Us
Trusthouse Forte
UBS Phillips & Drew
Unix
S.G. Warburg
Wartsila Marine (no umlauts)

Some other British and American company names are listed under
STOCK MARKET INDICES.

Crawford's Directory of City Connections (The Economist Books
and Directories, London) lists most big British companies, and
makes a point of spelling their names using each one's preferred
style.

COMPARE: A is compared **with** B when you draw attention to the
difference. A is compared **to** B when you want to stress their similar-
ity ("Shall I compare thee to a summer's day?")

COMPLAISANT people aim to please others; if they are **compla-
cent**, they are pleased with themselves.

COMPOUND does not mean **make worse**. It may mean **combine**
or, intransitively, **agree** or **come to terms**. To **compound a felony**
means to **agree for a consideration not to prosecute**.

COMPRISE means **is composed of. The Democratic coalition
comprises women, workers, blacks and Jews. Women make up**
(not comprise) **three-fifths of the Democratic coalition.** Alter-
natively, **Three-fifths of the Democratic coalition is composed
of women.**

CONTINUOUS describes something uninterrupted; **continual**
admits of a break. If your neighbours play loud music every night, it
is a **continual nuisance**; but it isn't a **continuous nuisance** unless
the music is never turned off.

CONVINCE. Don't **convince** people **to** do something. In that context the word you want is **persuade**. **The prime minister was persuaded to call a June election; he was convinced of the wisdom of doing so only after he had won.**

COUNTRIES AND THEIR INHABITANTS.

In most contexts sacrifice precision to simplicity and use **Britain** rather than **Great Britain** or the **United Kingdom,** and **America** rather than the **United States of America.** ("In all pointed sentences some degree of accuracy must be sacrificed to conciseness." Dr Johnson.) (See also pages 133ff.)

The **Soviet Union** used often to be called **Russia,** particularly in foreign-policy contexts. But nowadays it is usually important to recognise that Russia is only one of the 12 republics that make up the disintegrating country, which should therefore be given its full name, the **Soviet Union.** That country is (late 1991) without a satisfactory name: the **Soviet Union** is no longer officially approved of, but the recommended alternative, the **Union of Sovereign States,** means nothing to most people and has no obvious adjective. For the moment, therefore, refer to what used to be the Soviet Union (minus **Estonia, Latvia** and **Lithuania)** as the **former Soviet Union** or **ex-Soviet Union** on first mention. Thereafter, drop former or ex-. The adjective has to be **Soviet.** Avoid, however, calling the people of the Soviet Union **Soviets,** which as a noun should be confined to references to councils. Letting inaccuracy triumph over ugliness, you may call Soviet citizens **Russians,** unless precision demands that you call them **Soviet citizens** or **people, Uzbeks, Tajiks, Azerbaijanis,** etc.

It is sometimes important to be precise in other contexts. Remember therefore that **Great Britain** consists of **England, Scotland** and **Wales,** which together with **Northern Ireland** (which we generally call **Ulster,** though Ulster strictly includes three counties in the republic of Ireland) make up the **United Kingdom.**

Ireland is simply **Ireland.** Although it is a republic, it is not the Republic of Ireland. Neither is it, in English, Eire.

Remember, too, that although it is usually all right to talk about the inhabitants of the United States as **Americans,** the term also applies to everyone from Canada to Cape Horn. It may be necessary to write **United States citizens.** Do not, however, use **US,** except where it is part of a company's name, when it should be small caps.

In all cases it is best to refer to the specific nationality: thus **Canadians** rather than **North Americans;** never **Asians.**

CREDIBLE means to be believable; credulous means too ready to believe. **Her explanation for missing the meeting was credible. His explanation that he found the money at the end of the rainbow convinced only the credulous.**

CRISIS. This is a decisive event or turning-point. Many of the economic and political troubles wrongly described as **crises** are really **persistent difficulties, sagas** or **affairs**.

CURRENCIES. Use $ as the standard currency and in general convert currencies to $ on first mention.

Britain

1p, 2p, 3p, to **99p** (*not* £0.99)
£6 (*not* £6.00)
£5,000–6,000 (*not* £5,000–£6,000)

£5m–6m(*not* £5m–£6m)
£5 billion–6 billion
 (*not* £5–6 billion)

A **billion** is a thousand million, a **trillion** is a thousand billion. See also FIGURES, MEASUREMENT and MEASURES (Part III, pages 115ff).

America
$ will do generally. Spell out **cents**.

A$, C$, HK$, M$, NT$, NZ$ and **S$** are Australian, Canadian, Hong Kong, Malaysian, New Taiwanese, New Zealand and Singapore $ or dollars. Other currencies are **DM, BFr, FFr, SFr, IR£** (punts), **ASch, Ptas, SDR, DKr** (Danish krone, kroner), **NKr** (Norwegian krone, kroner), **SKr** (Swedish krona, kronor) and **¥**. With all these, write the abbreviation followed by the figure: **¥100** (not 100 yen), **Ptas100** (not 100 pesetas), **SDR1m** (not 1m SDRs).

Sums in other currencies, including the **ecu**, are written in full, with the number first: **100m ecus, 100m escudos, 100m guilders, 100m kwacha, 100m lire** (if Italian, **liras** if Turkish), **100m naira, 100m pesos, 100m rand** (not rands), **100m rupees** and **100m yuan** (not renminbi).

Currencies are not set in small caps, unless they occur as words in text without figures attached: **He who pays the piper, whether in D-marks or SDRs, calls the tune.**

For a full list of currencies, with currency symbols (included for reference, not necessarily for use), see pages 101ff.

CURRENT and **contemporary** mean **at that time**, not necessarily **at this time.** So a series of **current prices** from 1960 to 1970 will not be in **today's prices**, just as **contemporary art** in 1800 was not **modern art**.

D

DATES. Month, day, year, in that order, with no commas:

July 5th	1980s
July 5th 1997	Monday July 5th
July 5th–12th 1997	July 27th–August 3rd 1997
July 1997	1997–98

Write out
20th century, 21st century   20th-century ideas
but
a man in his 20s, and 20th anniversary.

In general give dates; **last week** or **last month** can cause confusion.
    Write **the second world war** or **the 1939–45 war**, not **world war II** or **2**. Similarly, prefer **the first world war** to **world war I** or **1**. **Post-war** and **pre-war** are hyphenated.
    See also FIGURES and HYPHENS.

DECIMATE means to destroy a proportion (originally a tenth) of a group of people or things, not to destroy them all or nearly all.

DEFINITIVE means authoritative, final, decisive; **definite** means precise, distinct.

DELIVER is transitive. So if someone is to **deliver,** he must deliver **letters, babies** or **the goods** – whether **groceries** or **what he promised.**

DEPRECATE means to **express disapproval of;** depreciate means to **belittle** or **reduce the value of. They deprecated his violent language but did not wish to depreciate the importance of his message.**

DIFFERENT from, not **to** or **than.**

DILEMMA. This is not just any old awkwardness, it is one with horns, being, properly, a form of argument (the horned syllogism) in which you find yourself committed to accept one of two propositions each of which contradicts your original contention. Hence a dilemma offers the choice between two alternatives, each with equally nasty consequences.

DISINTERESTED means **impartial**; **uninterested** means **bored**. ("Disinterested curiosity is the lifeblood of civilisation." G.M. Trevelyan.)

DISTINCTIVE means **characteristic, serving to identify**; **distinct** means **definite, distinguishable, separate**. Entering his room, she noticed that, as well as the distinctive smell of the cigars he always smoked, there was a faint but distinct odour of rotting fish.

DUE TO has three meanings:
1. caused by, as in **The cancellation, due to rain, of ...** In this sense, it must follow a noun, so do not write **The match was cancelled due to rain**. If you mean **because of** and for some reason are reluctant to say it, you probably want **owing to**. **It was cancelled owing to rain** is all right.
2. owed to, as in **A month's salary is due to Smith**.
3. arranged or timed to, as in **The meeting is due to end at 3.30**.

E

-EABLE. See -ABLE.

EARNINGS: do not write **earnings** when you mean **profits** (say if they are operating, gross, pre-tax or net).

-EE: **employees, evacuees, detainees, referees, refugees** but, please, no **attendees** (those attending), **draftees** (conscripts), **escapees** (escapers) or **retirees** (the retired).

EFFECT means to **accomplish**, so **The novel effected a change in his attitude**. See also AFFECT.

EFFECTIVELY means **with effect**; if you mean **in effect**, say it. **The matter was effectively dealt with on Friday** means it was **done well** on Friday. **The matter was, in effect, dealt with on Friday** means that it was **more or less attended to** on Friday. **Effectively leaderless** would do as a description of the demonstrators in East Germany in 1989 but not those in Tiananmen Square.

ENORMITY means a **crime, sin** or **monstrous wickedness. The enormity of his crime** is tautologous.

EPICENTRE means that point on the earth's surface above the centre of an earthquake. To say that **Mr Ridley was at the epicentre of the dispute** suggests that the argument took place underground.

ETHNIC GROUPS. Avoid giving offence. This should be your first concern. But also avoid mealy-mouthed euphemisms and terms that have not generally caught on despite promotion by pressure-groups. If and when it becomes plain that American blacks no longer wish to be called **black**, as some years ago it became plain that they no

longer wished to be called **coloured**, then call them **African-American** (or whatever). Till then they are **blacks**.

When writing about Spanish-speaking people in the United States, use either **Latino** or **Hispanic** as a general term, but try to be specific (eg, Mexican-American).

Africans may be black or white. If you mean blacks, write **blacks**. People of mixed race in South Africa are **Coloureds**.

The inhabitants of **Azerbaijan** are **Azerbaijanis**, some of whom, but not all, are **Azeris**. Those **Azeris** who live in other places, such as Nakhichevan, are not **Azerbaijanis**.

Anglo-Saxon is not a synonym for English-speaking.

See also STATES, Part III, pages 133ff.

EVERY ONE refers to a number; **everyone** means **everybody**.

Ex. Be careful with **ex**: a **Liberal ex-member** has lost his seat; **an ex-Liberal member** has lost his party.

EXCEPTIONABLE means can be taken exception to; **exceptional** means unusual, out of the ordinary. To claim that there has been no musical genius since Beethoven is an exceptionable remark, as there have been many other exceptional composers.

F

FEWER (not less) than seven speeches, fewer than seven samurai. Use **fewer**, not **less**, with numbers of individual items or people. **Less than £200, less than 700 tonnes of oil, less than a third,** because these are measured quantities or proportions, not individual items.

FIEF, not fiefdom.

FIGURES.

Never start a sentence with a figure; write the number in words instead.

Use figures for numerals from 11 upwards, and for all numerals that include a decimal point or a fraction (eg, **4.25, 4¼**). Use words for simple numerals from one to ten, except: in references to pages; in percentages (eg, **4%**); and in sets of numerals some of which are higher than ten, eg, **Deaths from this cause in the past three years were 14, 9 and 6.**

Fractions should be hyphenated (**two-thirds, five-eighths,** etc) and, unless they are attached to whole numbers (**8⅔, 29⅝**), spelled out in words, even when the figures are higher than ten: **He gave a tenth of his salary to the church, a twentieth to his mistress and a thirtieth to his wife.** See also FRACTIONS, page 108.

Do not compare a fraction with a decimal (so avoid **The rate fell from 3½% to 3.1%**).

Fractions are more precise than decimals (3.14 neglects an infinity of figures that are embraced by $^{22}/_7$), but your readers probably do not think so. You should therefore use fractions for rough figures (**Kenya's population is growing at 3½% a year, A hectare is 2½ acres**) and decimals for more exact ones: **The retail price index is rising at an annual rate of 10.6%.**

Use **m** for **million.** But spell out **billion,** which to us means 1,000m, except in charts, where **bn** is permissible. Thus: **8m, £8m, 8 billion, DM8 billion.**

Use **5,000–6,000, 5–6%, 5m–6m** (not **5–6m**) and also **5 billion– 6 billion** or **5bn–6bn.** But **sales rose from 5m to 6m** (not **5m–6m**); **estimates ranged between 5m and 6m** (not **5m–6m**).

Where **to** is being used as part of a ratio, it is usually best to spell it out. Thus **They decided, by nine votes to two, to put the matter to the general assembly which voted, 27 to 19, to insist that the ratio of vodka to tomato juice in a bloody mary should be at least one to three, though the odds of this being so in most bars** were put at no better than **11 to 4**. Where a ratio is being used adjectivally, figures and hyphens may be used, but only if one of the figures is greater than ten: thus **a 50-20 vote, a 19-9 vote**. Otherwise, spell out the figures and use **to: a two-to-one vote, a ten-to-one likelihood**.

Do not use a hyphen or dash in place of **to** except with figures: **He received a sentence of 15–20 years in jail** but **He promised to have escaped within three to four weeks' time**.

Avoid **from 1947–50** (say **in 1947–50** or **from 1947 to 1950**) and **between 1961–65** (say **in 1961–65** or **from 1961 to 1965**).

With figures, use **a person** or **per person, a year** or **per year**, not **per caput, per capita** or **per annum**.

The style for aircraft types can be confusing. Some have hyphens in obvious places (eg, **DC-10**, **Mirage F-1E**, **Mig-21**), some in unusual places (**BAC 1-11**) and some none at all (**BAe 146**, **TriStar**). Others have both name and number (**Lockheed P-3 Orion**). When in doubt, use Jane's "All The World's Aircraft". Its index also includes makers' correct names.

The style for calibres is **50mm** or **105mm** with no hyphen, but **5.5-inch** and **25-pounder**.

Use the sign **%** instead of **per cent**. But write **percentage**, not **%age** (though in most contexts **proportion** or **share** is preferable).

See also HYPHENS, MEASUREMENTS, MEASURES (Part III, page 115ff).

FINALLY: do not use **finally** when, at the end of a series, you mean **lastly** or, in other contexts, when you mean **at last**. **Richard Burton finally marries Liz Taylor** would have been all right second time round but not first.

FLAUNT means **display**; **flout** means **disdain**. If you **flout** this distinction you will **flaunt** your ignorance.

FOREIGN WORDS AND PHRASES. Try not to use foreign words and phrases unless there is no English alternative, which is unusual (so **a year** or **per year**, not **per annum**; **a person** or **per person** not **per capita**; **beyond one's authority** not **ultra vires**; etc). See also ITALICS.

FORGO means **do without**; it foregoes the **e**. **Forego** means **go before**.

FORMER: avoid wherever possible use of **the former** and **the latter**. It usually causes confusion.

FORTUITOUS means **accidental**, not **fortunate** or **well-timed**.

FRACTIOUS means **peevish** or **unruly**; factious means **divisive** or **produced by faction. English soccer fans have a reputation for being both fractious and factious.**

FRANKENSTEIN was not a monster, but his creator.

FUND is a technical term, meaning to **convert floating debt into more or less permanent debt at fixed interest.** Do not use it if you mean to **finance** or to **pay for.**

G

GENDER is a word to be applied to grammar, not people. If someone is female, that is her **sex** not her **gender**.

GENTLEMEN'S AGREEMENT, not gentleman's.

GENERATION: take care. You can be a second-generation Frenchman, but if you are a second-generation immigrant that means you have left the country your parents came to.

GET: an adaptable verb, but it has its limits. A man does not **get** sacked or promoted, he **is** sacked or promoted.

H

HALVE is a transitive verb, so deficits can double but not **halve**. They must **fall by half**.

HANGING CLAUSES. If you begin a sentence with an adjectival or adverbial phrase, make sure that it qualifies the subject of the sentence. Thus, avoid: **After a fortnight's absence, your house plants will have shrivelled up.**

HEALTHY. If you think something is **desirable** or **good**, say so. Do not call it **healthy**.

HOBSON'S CHOICE is not **the lesser of two evils**, it is **no choice at all**.

HOI POLLOI means **the many** or **the rabble** in Greek. Do not therefore write **the hoi polloi**.

HOMOGENEOUS means **of the same kind or nature**. Homogenous means **similar because of common descent**.

HOMOSEXUAL: since this word comes from the Greek word *homos* (same), not the Latin word *homo* (man), it applies as much to women as to men. It is therefore as daft to write **Homosexuals and lesbians** as to write **People and women**.

HOPEFULLY: by all means begin an article hopefully, but never write: **Hopefully, it will be finished by Wednesday.** Try: **With luck, if all goes well, it is hoped that ...**

HYPHENS.
Use hyphens as follows.
But "If you take hyphens seriously, you will surely go mad." (Oxford University Press style manual).

1. Fractions (whether nouns or adjectives): **two-thirds, four-fifths, one-sixth**, etc. (See also FRACTIONS, Part III, page 108.)

2. Most words that begin with prefixes like **ex** (q.v.), **anti, non** and **neo**. Thus, **anti-aircraft, anti-fascist, anti-submarine** (but anti-climax, antidote, antiseptic); **non-combatant, non-existent, non-payment, non-violent** (but nonaligned, nonconformist, non-

plussed, nonstop); **neo-conservative, neo-liberal** (but neoclassicism, neolithic, neologism).

A sum followed by the word **worth** also needs a hyphen: thus, **$25m-worth of goods**.

3. Some titles:

	but
vice-president	
director-general	deputy director
under-secretary	deputy secretary
secretary-general	district attorney
attorney-general	general secretary
lieutenant-colonel	
major-general	

4. To avoid ambiguities:

a little-used car	a little used-car
cross-complaint	cross complaint
high-school girl	high schoolgirl

fine-tooth comb (most people do not comb their teeth)

5. Aircraft:

DC-10	**Mirage F-1E**
Lockheed P-3 Orion	**Mig-23**

(If in doubt, consult Jane's "All the World's Aircraft".)

6. Adjectives formed from two or more words:
right-wing groups (*but* **the right wing** of the party)
balance-of-payments difficulties
private-sector wages
public-sector borrowing requirement
a 70-year-old judge
value-added tax (VAT)

7. Adverbs do not need to be linked to participles or adjectives by hyphens in simple constructions: **The regiment was ill equipped for its task; The principle is well established; Though expensively educated, the journalist knew no grammar.** But if the adverb is one of two words together being used adjectivally, a hyphen is needed: **The ill-equipped regiment was soon repulsed; All well-established principles should be periodically challenged; Never employ an expensively-educated journalist.** See ADVERBS.

8. Do not overdo the literary device of hyphenating words that are not usually linked: the stringing-together-of-lots-and-lots-of-words-and-ideas tendency can be tiresome.

9. Separating identical letters: **book-keeping** (but **bookseller**), **coat-tails, co-operate, unco-operative, pre-eminent, pre-empt** (but **predate, precondition**), **re-emerge, re-entry, trans-ship**.
But **rearrange, reborn, repurchase**.
Exceptions also include **override, overrule, underrate, withhold**.

10. Nouns formed from prepositional verbs: **build-up, call-up, get-together, round-up, set-up, shake-up**, etc.

11. The quarters of the compass: **north-east(ern), south-east(ern), south-west(ern), north-west(ern), the mid-west(ern)**.

12. Makers, miners, workers can stand unattached and hyphenless: **car maker, coal miner, steel worker**. But **policy-makers, policy-making**.

13. *One word*

airfield	lacklustre	stockmarket
backlog	loophole	strongman
bilingual	lopsided	subcommittee
blackboard	machinegun	subcontinent
blueprint	multilingual	subcontract
businessman	nevertheless	subhuman
bypass	nonetheless	submachinegun
ceasefire	offshore	sunbelt
coastguard	onshore	takeover
comeback	overpaid	taskforce
commonsense (adj)	overrated	threshold
foothold	override	turnout
forever	overrule	underdog
goodwill	peacekeepers (-ing)	underpaid
halfhearted	petrochemical	underrated
handout	profitmaking	videocassette
handpicked	salesforce	videodisc
hardline	seabed	wartime
hijack	shipbuilders	workforce
hobnob	shipbuilding	worldwide
kowtow	soyabean	worthwhile

14. *Two words*

air base	ballot box	common sense
air force	car maker	(noun)
aircraft carrier	chip maker	drug dealer (-ing)
arm's length	coal miner	errand boy

girl friend
microchip maker
oil field
on to

place name
rain forest
steel maker
steel worker

under way
vice versa

15. *Two hyphenated words*

build-up
death-squads
drawing-board
faint-hearted
fig-leaf, (*but* other leaves are un-hyphenated)
fund-raiser (-ing)
hot-head
ice-cream
infra-red

know-how
mid-week, mid-August, etc
multi-party
policy-makers (-ing), *but* foreign-policy makers (-ing)
post-war
pre-war
pull-out (noun)

re-present (*meaning* present again)
re-sort (*meaning* sort again)
starting-point
sticking-point
think-tank
time-bomb
turning-point
working-party

16. *Three words*

capital gains tax
chiefs of staff
in as much
in so far

Three hyphenated words

brother-in-law
chock-a-block
commander-in-chief
no-man's-land
prisoners-of-war
second-in-command

17. Avoid **from 1947–50** (say **in 1947–50** or **from 1947 to 1950**) and **between 1961–65** (say **in 1961–65** or **from 1961 to 1965**). Some people use dashes, not hyphens, with dates. A hyphen (or dash) should not be used instead of **to** except with figures. See also DATES, FIGURES.

HYPOTHERMIA is what kills old folk in winter. If you say it is **hyperthermia**, that means they have been carried off by heat stroke.

I

-IBLE. See -ABLE.

ILK means **same**, so of that ilk means **of the place of the same name as the family**, not **of that kind**. Best avoided.

IMMOLATE means to **sacrifice**, not to **burn**.

IMPORTANT: if something is important, say why and to whom. Use sparingly.

INCHOATE means **not fully developed** or **at an early stage**, and not **incoherent** or **chaotic**.

INFER. By including this word, we **imply** that it is sometimes misused. When reading this entry, you **infer** that the two highlighted words have different meanings.

INITIALS. Initials in people's names, or in companies named after them, take points (with a space between initials and name, but not between initials). Thus, **F.W. de Klerk, E.I. Du Pont de Nemours, F.W. Woolworth**. The only exceptions are for PEOPLE, COMPANIES and ORGANISATIONS that deliberately leave the points out, eg, **UBS Phillips & Drew**. In general, follow the practice preferred by themselves in writing their own names. See also ABBREVIATIONS.

INTERNMENT. Generally considered a preferable penalty to **interment**: the former means **confinement**, the latter means **burial** in a grave or tomb.

INVESTIGATIONS of, not **into**.

ITALICS. Use italics for:
1. Foreign words and phrases, such as *cabinet* (French type), *de jure, glasnost, intifada, Mitbestimmung, papabile, perestroika, tolkach, ujamaa* unless they are so familiar that they have become anglicised. Thus **ad hoc, apartheid, machismo, putsch, pogrom, status quo**, etc, are in roman. Make sure that the meaning of any foreign word you use is clear; and give it its correct accent. See also ACCENTS; ANIMALS, PLANTS, ETC; FOREIGN WORDS AND PHRASES.

2. Newspapers and periodicals. Note that only *The Economist* and *The Times* have **The** italicised. Thus the *Daily Telegraph,* the *New York Times*, the *Observer*, the *Spectator*, the *Financial Times* (but *Le Monde, Die Welt, Die Zeit*). Books, pamphlets, plays, radio and television programmes are roman, with capital letters for each main word, in quotation marks. Thus: **"Pride and Prejudice"**, **"Much Ado about Nothing"**, **"Any Questions"**, **"Crossfire"**, etc. But the **Bible** and its books (**Genesis, Ecclesiastes, John,** etc) do not have inverted commas. These rules apply to footnotes as well as bodymatter.

However, book publishers generally use italics for books and pamphlets, plays, radio and television programmes.

3. Lawsuits. If abbreviated, *versus* should always be shortened to *v*, with no point after it. Thus: **Brown** *v* **Board of Education, Coatsworth** *v* **Johnson**.

4. The names of ships, aircraft, spacecraft. Thus: HMS *Illustrious, Spirit of St Louis, Challenger,* etc.
Note that a ship is **she**; a country is **it**.

5. But *The Economist* does not use italics in titles or captions.

J · K

JARGON. Avoid it. All sections of *The Economist* should be intelligible to all our readers, most of whom are foreigners. You may have to think harder if you are not to use jargon, but you can still be precise. Technical terms should be used in their proper context; do not use them out of it. In many instances simple words can do the job of **exponential** (try **fast**), **interface** (**frontier** or **border**), and so on. Avoid, above all, meaningless or ambiguous jargon.

•

KEY: keys may be **major** or **minor**, but not **low**. Few of the decisions, people, industries described as **key** are truly **indispensable**, and fewer still **open locks**.

KNOWLEDGEABLE: verbs are -able, but not nouns. Try **well informed**.

L

LAST: the **last** issue of *The Economist* implies our extinction; prefer **last week's** issue, the **previous** issue. Likewise avoid the **last** issue of *Foreign Affairs*: prefer the **latest, current,** or (eg) **June** issue, or **this month's** or **last month's** issue.

Last year, in 1991, means 1990; if you mean the 12 months up to the time of writing, write **the past year.** The same goes for the **past** month, **past** week, **past** (not **last**) ten years. See also DATES.

LEEWAY is **leeward drift,** not space to do a bit of manoeuvring in.

LIFESTYLE: prefer **way of life.**

LIGHT-YEAR. A light-year is a measurement of distance, not of time. It is the approximate distance travelled by light in one year.

Thus: 1 light-year $= 5.88 \times 10^{12}$ miles
$= 9.46 \times 10^{12}$ km

LOCATE, in all its forms, can usually be replaced by something less ugly. **The missing scientist was located** means he was **found. The diplomats will meet at a secret location** means either that they will meet **in a secret place** or that they will meet **secretly. A company located in Texas** is simply **a company in Texas.**

LOWER CASE. See CAPITALS.

LUXURIANT means growing profusely, yielding in abundance; do not confuse with **luxurious.** Weeds are luxuriant, rare orchids luxurious.

M

MASTERFUL means **imperious**. Masterly means **skilled**.

MAXIMISE means **to make as great as possible. Weight-lifting can maximise your biceps, but not your health.**

MAY and **might** are not always interchangeable, and you may want **may** more often than you think. If in doubt, try **may** first.

You need **might** in the past tense. **I may go to Leeds later** becomes, in the past, **I might have gone to Leeds later**. And in indirect past speech it becomes **I said I might go to Leeds later.**

Conditional sentences using the subjunctive also need **might**. Thus **If I were to go to Leeds, I might have to stand all the way.** This could be rephrased **If I go to Leeds, I may have to stand all the way.** Conditional sentences stating something contrary to fact, however, need **might: If pigs had wings, birds might raise their eyebrows.**

Do not write **George Bush might be president of the United States, but he does not eat broccoli.** It should be **George Bush may be president of the United States, but he does not eat broccoli.** Only if you are putting forward a hypothesis that may or may not be true are **may** and **might** interchangeable. Thus **If Dan Quayle always eats his broccoli, he may** (or **might**) **become president of the United States.**

MEASUREMENTS. In most contexts that are not American or British, prefer **hectares** to **acres**, **kilometres** (or **km**) to **miles**, **metres** to **yards**, **litres** to **gallons**, **kilos** to **lb**, **tonnes** to **tons**, **Celsius** to **Fahrenheit**, etc. Regardless of which you choose, you should give an equivalent, on first use, in the other units: **It was hoped that after improvements to the engine the car would give 20km to the litre (47 miles per American gallon) compared with its present average of 15km per litre.**

Remember that in few countries do you now buy petrol in imperial gallons. In America it is sold in American gallons; in most places it is sold in litres.

See also MEASURES, page 115ff.

MEDIA: prefer **press and television** or, if the context allows it, just **press**. If you have to use the **media**, remember it is plural.

METAPHORS. "A newly invented metaphor assists thought by evoking a visual image," said George Orwell, "while on the other hand a metaphor which is technically 'dead' (eg, iron resolution) has in effect reverted to being an ordinary word and can generally be used without loss of vividness. But in between these two classes there is a huge dump of wornout metaphors which are merely used because they save people the trouble of inventing phrases for themselves."

A recent issue of *The Economist* contained these metaphors.

a trail of crushed rivals
billing and cooing politicians
a smaller helping of Europe's manifest destiny
a project falling at the first hurdle
a weaker grip on monetary policy
a track record on inflation
tabloid reporters lapping up stories
a report leaving the door ajar
irresistible forces in the Soviet Union about to meet an immovable object
an enormous roadblock in the path of reform
investors crying foul
a behind-the-scenes collapse of companies
Mr Bush's U-turn
the congressional pork barrel
water off a duck's back in the Senate
a door slammed shut in China
a blind eye turned in Taiwan
an investor jumping the gun
heat off in America

the reins of power in Japan
a bargaining chip in South Africa
a honeymoon (soon to be over)
an iron-clad argument
Soviet foot-dragging
a run-up to the Italian presidency
a counterweight to German domination
heavy-handed carpet-baggers
a shadow cast over Poland's future
bureaucratic barriers
uprooted democracy
grass-roots organisations
mainstream conservatives
young turks
a leading wet
a crash-course in capitalism
grinding poverty in East Germany
flabby banks getting into shape
politicians turning a deaf ear
a binge of brand acquisitions
Philip Morris gobbling up United Biscuits.

Some of these are tired, and will therefore tire the reader. Most are so exhausted that they may be considered dead, and are therefore permissible. But use all metaphors, dead or alive, sparingly, otherwise you will make trouble for yourself. (See also CLICHES.)

The same issue of *The Economist* had a **package cutting the budget deficit, the administration loth to sign on to higher Gramm-Rudman targets, liberals accused of playing politics on the court (Supreme, not tennis),** only to find in the next sentence that **the boot was on the other foot, the lure of East**

Germany as a springboard to the struggling markets of Eastern Europe, West Europeanness helping to dilute an image, Mr Molyneux finding a pretext to stall the process before looking for a few integrationist crumbs, an end-of-millennium spring clean that became in the next sentence a stalking-horse for greater spending, and Michelin axing jobs in painful surgery in order stay at the top of a league table. Soon Mr Michelin was plunging his company even further in to debt, though if it were to stay afloat his ambitions would have to be deflated. Little wonder other French firms were striking out abroad. The reader had to go down to the seas again two pages on when a flotilla of mutual and quoted life-assurance outfits were confident of surviving turbulent waters. The galleons were afloat, but the medium-sized and smaller mutuals quickly turned into fodder for domestic and foreign predators. Further on, banks going to the altar in the expectation of a tax-free dowry saw it become a sweetener in the next sentence and the bill that delivered it transformed into a panacea. Those who wanted to learn about Japanese equity financing were told of a stockmarket crawling back (not on its feet, it was explained) towards its old high, of commercial banks keeping the wolf from the door and, three paragraphs later, of the stockmarket's double whammy. One whammy was a crash which made a big dent in shares, the other blew a hole (a gaping one) in the so-called *tokkin* funds. On, on went the reader past masked bunglings, key measures, money-supply growth out of hand, a haunted Bank of Japan redoubling its squeeze, banks slashing growth lest they found themselves on a tight leash before being cracked down on. Few could have been surprised to learn at the end of the article that another dose of higher interest rates might be forced on the banks if the present inflationary symptoms turned into measles-like spots, and if the apothecaries at the finance ministry agreed with the diagnosis.

These two sentences written by a staff member were not published:

But Ireland, Greece, Spain and Portugal are not satisfied and hint that they may not swallow the pill of EMU without some sugar. Mr Major is trying to stitch up the unholiest of alliances, between anti-regional-aid Britain and a group of countries which fears any EMU unattached to a cushion of extra regional money.

These two sentences, used as an opening paragraph to arrest the attention of the readers of *A.N. Other* newspaper, found their way past its sub-editors and into print:

Bulgaria is on its knees. A long-simmering economic crisis has erupted, gripping the country in a fierce and unrelenting embrace.

METE. You may **mete out** punishment, but if it is to fit the crime it is **meet**.

MILLIONAIRE: the time has gone when girls in the Bois du Boulogne would think that the term **millionaire** adequately described the man who broke the Bank at Monte Carlo. If you wish to use it, make it plain that **millionaire** refers to income (in dollars or pounds), not to capital. Otherwise try **plutocrat** or **rich man**.

MINIMISE means to make as small as possible; you cannot **slightly minimise** something.

MITIGATES mollifies, **militates** does the opposite.

MOVE: do not use if you mean **decision**, **bid**, **deal** or something more precise. But **move** rather than **relocate**.

N

NAMES

CHINESE NAMES. In general follow the Pinyin spelling, which has replaced the old Wade-Giles system, except for people from the past, and people and places outside mainland China. **Peking** is therefore **Beijing** and **Mao** is **Zedong**, not **Tse-tung**.

There are no hyphens in Pinyin spelling. So:

Deng Xiaoping
Guangdong (ex-Kwangtung)
Guangzhou (ex-Canton)
Hu Yaobang
Jiang Qing (ex-Mrs Mao)
Mao Zedong (not Tse-tung)
Qingdao (ex-Tsingtao)
Tianjin (ex-Tientsin)
Xinjiang (ex-Sinkiang)
Zhao Ziyang

But
Chiang Kai-shek
Hong Kong
Li Ka-shing

The family name in China comes first, so **Deng Xiaoping** becomes **Mr Deng** on a later mention.

Names from **Singapore, Korea, Vietnam** have no hyphens: **Lee Kuan Yew, Ho Chi Minh**.

Some (not all) Indonesians have one name: **Mr Suharto**.

See also FOREIGN WORDS AND PHRASES; PEOPLE; TITLES.

DUTCH NAMES. If using first name and surname together, **vans** and **dens** are lower case: **Dries van Agt** and **Joop den Uyl**. But without their first names they become **Mr Van Agt** and **Mr Den Uyl**. This rule does not always apply to Dutch names in Belgium and South Africa.

FRENCH NAMES: generally follow French convention, capitalising **Le, La, Les, Du** and **Des**, but not **de** or **d'**.

GERMAN NAMES: **von** is lower case. But **Mr Otto Habsburg** (no von).

NONE usually takes a singular verb. So does **neither** (or **either**) **A nor B**, unless B is plural, as in **Neither the Dutchman nor the**

Danes have done it, where the verb agrees with the element closest to it.

NOR. This conjunction contains a negative – it means **and not** – and so it should not be used after a negative form of a verb.

NOT ONLY. This should appear next to the item it qualifies. **His sister loved not only him** and **his sister not only loved him** have different meanings. When used with **but also**, it must either follow the verb or the verb must be repeated, eg, **he not only hurt her feelings but also hurt her pride**, better phrased as **he hurt not only her feelings but also her pride** (see the advice given under BOTH ... AND).

NUMBERS. See FIGURES, MEASUREMENTS, MEASURES (Part III, page 115ff).

O

ONLY: put **only** as close as you can to the words it qualifies. Thus, **These animals mate only in June**. To say **They only mate in June** implies that in June they do nothing else.

OVERWHELM means **submerge utterly, crush, bring to sudden ruin**. Majority votes, for example, seldom do any of these things.

P

PEOPLE. Call them what they want to be called, short of festooning them with titles. Use full stops after initials.

Here are some names which may present problems.

Yasser Arafat
Hafez Assad
Omar el Bashir
Zine El Abidine Ben Ali
Chadli Benjedid
Alexander Bessmertnykh
Zbigniew Brzezinski
Leopoldo Calvo-Sotelo
Nicolae Ceausescu
Uncle Tom Cobbleigh
Poul Dalsager
Carlo De Benedetti
Gaston Defferre
Gianni De Michelis
Ciriaco De Mita
Carlo Ripa di Meana
Edward du Cann
Lawrence Eagleburger
King Fahd
Garret FitzGerald
Gandhi
Hans-Dietrich Genscher
Felipe Gonzalez
Mikhail Gorbachev
Gurkha
Denis Healey
Elias Hrawi
Saddam Hussein
Ahmad Khomeini

Hans-Jochen Vogel
Jeane Kirkpatrick
Helmut Kohl
Oskar Lafontaine
François Mitterrand
Daniel arap Moi
Hosni Mubarak
Muhammed (unless it is part
    of the name of someone who
    spells it differently)
Gaafar Numeiri
Edgard Pisani
Moammar Qaddafi
Karl Otto Pöhl
Yitzhak Rabin
Ali Akbar Rafsanjani
Edzard Reuter
Nikolai Ryzhkov
Andrei Sakharov
Ali Abdullah Saleh
Yitzhak Shamir
Edward Shevardnadze
George Shultz,
    Charles Schultze
Mario Soares (Portugal),
    Adolfo Suarez (Spain)
Alexander Solzhenitsyn
tsar
Caspar Weinberger

See also FOREIGN WORDS AND PHRASES; NAMES; SPELLING; TITLES.

PERCENTAGES. Use the sign % instead of **per cent** and write **percentage**, not **%age**. Write **5–6%**, not **5%–6%** or **5%–6**. See FIGURES.

PERCOLATE means to pass **through**, not **up** or **down**.

PERSPICACITY and **perspicuity** should be the twin aims of writers: an acuteness of understanding coupled with lucidity of expression.

PHASE: when discussing incomes policies, monetary unions, extended plans, etc, prefer **stage** to **phase**.

PHONE: short but not sweet. Use **telephone**.

PLACES. Use English forms when they are in common use: **Basle, Cologne, Leghorn, Lower Saxony, Lyons, Marseilles, Naples, Nuremberg, Turin**. And English rather than American – **Rockefeller Centre, Pearl Harbour** – unless the place name is part of a company name, such as **Rockefeller Center Properties Inc**. But follow local practice when a country expressly changes its name, or the names of rivers, towns, etc, within it. Thus **Chemnitz**, not **Karl-Marx-Stadt**; **Côte d'Ivoire**, not **Ivory Coast**; **Nizhny Novgorod**, not **Gorky**; **Myanmar**, not **Burma**; **Yangon**, not **Rangoon**; and **St Petersburg**, not **Leningrad**.

Do not use the definite article before **Lebanon, Piedmont, Punjab, Sudan, Transkei** and **Ukraine**, but it is **the Caucasus, The Gambia, The Hague, the Maghreb** – and **La Paz, Le Havre, Los Angeles**, etc. See also COUNTRIES AND THEIR INHABITANTS, and STATES, ETC, page 133.

Do not use the names of capital cities as synonyms for their governments. **Britain will send a gunboat** is fine, but **London will send a gunboat** suggests that this will be the action of the people of London alone. To write **Washington and Moscow now differ only in their approach to Havana** is absurd.

Although the place is **Western** (or **Eastern**) **Europe**, the people are **West** or **East Europeans**.

Here are the spellings of some common problematic place names.

Argentina (adj and people Argentine, *not* Argentinian)
Baden-Württemberg
Baghdad
Bahrain
Bangladesh
Basle
Belorussia
Bophuthatswana
Cameroon
Cape Town
Caribbean
Cincinnati
Colombia (South America)
Columbia (university, District of); British Columbia
Côte d'Ivoire (*not* Ivory Coast)
Cracow
Dar es Salaam
Djibouti
Dominica (Caribbean island)
Dominican Republic (part of another island)
El Salvador,
Salvadorean
The Gambia
Gettysburg
Gothenburg
Guatemala city
Gujarat, Gujarati
Guyana (*but* French Guiana)
Hanover
Harare
Hercegovina
Hong Kong (unless it is part of name of company which spells it as one

word: Hongkong
and Shanghai
Bank)
Jeddah
KaNgwane
Katmandu
Kazakhstan
Kirgizia
Kuwait city
KwaNdebele
KwaZulu
Luxembourg
Macau
Mauritania
Mexico City
Middlesbrough

Myanmar (*not*
Burma)
New York city
North Rhine-
Westphalia
Nuremberg
Panama city
Philippines (the
people are Filipinos
and Filipinas)
Phnom Penh
Pittsburgh
Quebec city
Quezon City
Reykjavik
Romania

Salzburg
Serbia (adj. Serb, *not*
Serbian)
Sri Lanka
St Antony's (college)
Strasbourg
Suriname
Taipei
Tajikistan
Teesside
Tehran
Uzbekistan
Valletta
Yugoslavia
Zurich

PLANE: this is a **tool**, a **surface** or sometimes, if it flies, it is an **aeroplane**, **aircraft** or **airliner** (not an **airplane**). **Warplane**, however, is allowed.

PLANTS: see ANIMALS, PLANTS, ETC.

PLURALS. No rules here. The spelling of the following plurals may be decided by either practice or derivation.

-oes

archipelagoes
buffaloes
cargoes
desperadoes
echoes
embargoes
grottoes
haloes

heroes
innuendoes
mementoes
mosquitoes
mottoes
noes
peccadilloes
potatoes

salvoes
tomatoes
tornadoes
torpedoes
vetoes
volcanoes

-os

Eskimos
altos
commandos
concertos
contraltos
dynamos
embryos
fiascos

folios
ghettos
impresarios
librettos
manifestos
oratorios
peccadillos
pianos

provisos
radios
silos
solos
sopranos
stilettos
studios
virtuosos

-ums
conundrums
crematoriums
forums
moratoriums

nostrums
quorums
referendums
stadiums

ultimatums
vacuums

-a
addenda
bacteria
consortia
corpora (plural of
  corpus)
corrigenda
crematoria

criteria
data
errata
genera (plural of
  genus)
media (but mediums
  communicate with

the spirit world)
memoranda
phenomena
quanta
sanatoria
strata

-uses
buses
caucuses
circuses

fetuses
focuses
geniuses

prospectuses

-i
alumni
bacilli
cacti

fungi
graffiti
nuclei

stimuli
termini

-s
agendas
arenas

milieus
panaceas

plateaus
quotas

-ae
amoebae
formulae

lacunae
nebulae

vertebrae

-ves
calves
hooves
scarves
sheaves
wharves

-fs
dwarfs
handkerchiefs
roofs
turfs

-eaus
bureaus (*but* bureaux de change)
tableaus
trousseaus

-eaux
châteaux

—es

amanuenses	bases	oases
analyses	crises	synopses
antitheses	hypotheses	

and indexes (of books); indices are indicators of index numbers; appendixes (anatomical variety; use appendices for literary sort).

PRECIPITOUS means **extremely steep**; a rash or hasty action is **precipitate**. **Precipitate share dealings led to a precipitous drop in prices.**

PREPOSITIONS at the end of sentences are permissible: **an example such as this is a good one to go by,** rather than **an example such as this is a good one by which to go.**

PRESENTLY means **soon**, not **at present**. **"Presently Kep opened the door of the shed, and let out Jemima Puddle-Duck."**

PREVARICATE means **evade the truth**; **procrastinate** means **put off.**

PRISTINE means in **original condition**, not **pure** or **clean**.

PROBLEM: the problem with problem is it is overused, so much so that it is becoming a problem word.

PROOF-READING

Look for errors in the following categories.

1. "Typos", which include misspelt words, punctuation mistakes, wrong numbers, transposed words or sentences.
2. Bad word breaks (see below).
3. Layout mistakes: wrongly positioned text (including captions, headings, folios, running heads) or illustrations, incorrect line spacing, missing items, widows (short lines at the top of a page).
4. Wrong fonts: errors in the use of italic, bold, etc.

Additionally, if the text contains cross-references to numbered pages or illustrations, the proof-reader is usually responsible for inserting the correct reference at page proof stage, and for checking cross-references.

The most effective way of proof-reading is to read the text several times, each time with a different focus, rather than attempting to carry out all checks in one go. This helps concentration and makes it easier to detect inconsistencies which are usually the sign of an error.

WORD BREAKS. If text is justified, or contains many long words, it may be necessary to break words, using a hyphen, at the end of lines. The aim should be to make these breaks as undisruptive as possible, so that the reader does not stumble or falter. Whenever possible, the word should be broken so that, helped by the context, the reader can successfully anticipate the whole word from the part of it given before the break. Here are some useful principles for deciding how to break a word.

1. Words that are already hyphenated should be broken at the hyphen, not given a second hyphen.
2. Words can be broken according to either their derivation (the British convention) or their pronunciation (the US convention): thus, **aristo-cracy** (UK) or **aristoc-racy** (US), **melli-fluous** (UK) or **mellif-luous** (US). See PART II for American usage.
3. Words of one syllable should not be broken.
4. Words of five or fewer characters should not be broken.
5. At least three characters must be taken over to the next line.
6. Words should not be broken so that their identity is confused or their identifying sound is distorted: thus, avoid **wo-men,** or **fo-ist.**
7. Personal names should not be broken.
8. Figures should not be broken or separated from their unit of measurement.
9. A word formed with a prefix or suffix should be broken at that point: thus, **bi-furcated, ante-diluvian, convert-ible.**
10. If a breakable word contains a double consonant, split it at that point: thus, **as-sess, ship-ping, prob-lem.**

PROOF-READING MARKS. Standard proof-reading marks are illustrated on the following pages. The intention of these marks is to identify, precisely and concisely, the nature of an error and, when necessary, the correction required. When corrections are extensive or complex, it is usually better to spell out, in full, the correct form of the text rather than leave the typesetter to puzzle over a string of hieroglyphs, however immaculately drawn and ordered. Be careful, though, to use capital letters and lower case as appropriate; mark all proof corrections clearly, keeping all letters separate, and write them in the margin in the order in which they fall on the line.

Instruction	Textual mark	Marginal mark & notes
Correction is concluded	None	/ Make after each correction
Leave unchanged	• • • • • • • • • under characters to remain	stet
Remove extraneous marks	Encircle marks to be removed	X eg, film or paper edges visible between lines on bromide proofs
Push down risen spacing material	Encircle blemish	⊥
Refer to appropriate authority anything of doubtful accuracy	Encircle word(s) affected	(?)
Insert in text the matter indicated in the margin	⋀ (caret mark)	New matter followed by ⋀
Insert additional matter identified by a letter in a diamond	⋀	Followed by for example Ⓐ	The relevant section of the copy should be supplied with the corresponding letter marked on it in a diamond, eg Ⓐ
Delete	/ through character(s) or ⊢——⊣ through words to be deleted	⌀
Delete and close up	⫯ through character(s) or ⊢⟜⟞⊣ through characters, eg, charaacter, charaaacter	⌒ ⌀ ⌣

Instruction	Textual mark	Marginal mark & notes
Close up – delete space	⌒	⌒
Substitute character or substitute part of one or more word(s)	through character / or ⊢——⁄ through words	new character or new word(s)
Wrong font Replace by characters of correct font	Encircle character(s) to be changed	⊗ or w.f.
Correct damaged character(s)	Encircle character(s) to be changed	✕
Set in or change to roman type	Encircle character(s) to be changed	Rom.
Set in or change to italic	——— under character(s) to to be set or changed	ital.
Set in or change to capital letters	═══ under character(s) to be set or changed	≡ or caps.
Set in or change to small capital letters	═══ under character(s) to be set or changed	═ or s.c.
Set in or change to capital letters for initial letters and small capital letters for the rest of the words	≡ under initial letters ═ under rest of word(s)	═══
Set in or change to bold type	∿∿∿ under character(s) to be set or changed	∿∿ or bold
Set in or change to bold italic type	∿∿∿ under character(s) to be set or changed	∿
Change capital letters to lower case letters	Encircle character(s) to be changed	≢ or l.c.

Instruction	Textual mark	Marginal mark & notes
Invert type	Encircle character to be changed	↺
Substitute or insert character in "superior" position	/ through character or ⋏ where required	Y under character e.g. ²⃒
Substitute or insert character in "inferior" position	/ through character or ⋏ where required	⋏ over character e.g. ⋏₂
Substitute ligature e.g. ffi for separate letters	⊢————⊣ through characters affected	⌒⌃⌄ e.g. ffi
Substitute separate letters for ligature	⊢————⊣	Write out separate letters
Substitute or insert full stop or decimal point	/ through character or ⋏ where required	⊙/
Substitute or insert colon	/ through character or ⋏ where required	⊙/
Substitute or insert semi-colon	/ through character or ⋏ where required	⁏
Insert space	⋏	# ⋏
Equal space	‖ between words or letters	equal # /
Reduce space	‖ between words or letters	less # /

Instruction	Textual mark	Marginal mark & notes
Substitute or insert oblique	/ through character or ⋀ where required	
Start new paragraph	[	n.p.
Run on (no new paragraph)	⌒	⌒
Transpose characters or words	between characters or words, numbered when necessary	and/or trs.
Transpose a number of characters or words	3 2 1 | | |	1 2 3 The vertical strokes are made through the characters or words to be transposed and numbered in the correct sequence
Transpose lines		
Transpose a number of lines	————3 ————2 ————1	Rules extend from the margin into the text with each line to be transplanted numbered in the correct sequence
Centre	⌈enclosing matter to be centred⌉	[ ]
Indent or move to the right		Give the amount of the indent in the marginal mark
Move to the left		Give the amount of the indent in the marginal mark
Abbreviation or figure to be spelt out in full	Encircle matter to be altered	spell out
Insert single or double quotes	⋀ ⋀	

57

PROPER NOUNS: if they have adjectives, use them. Thus a Californian (not **California**) judge, the **Pakistani** (not **Pakistan**) government, the **Texan** (not **Texas**) press.

PROTAGONIST means the **chief actor** or **combatant**. If you are referring to several people, they cannot all be protagonists.

PROTEST. Objectors protest that a decision is unfair, or they protest at or against it. **Employers have protested against the examination boards' decision to take no account of spelling in A-level marking systems** is right; **The NUT protested the penalisation of children from ethnic minorites for writing poor English** is wrong.

PRY: use **prise**, unless you mean **peer**.

PUNCTUATION

APOSTROPHES. Use the normal possessive ending **'s** after singular words or names that end in **s**: **boss's, caucus's, Delors's, St James's, Jones's.** Use it after plurals that do not end in **s**: **children's, Frenchmen's, media's.**

Use the ending **s'** on plurals that end in **s** – **Danes', bosses', Joneses'** – including plural names that take a singular verb, eg, **Reuters', Barclays', Stewarts & Lloyds', Salomon Brothers'.**

Although singular in other respects, the United States, the United Nations, the Philippines, etc, have a plural possessive apostrophe: eg, **What will the United States' next move be?**

People's = of (the) people.

Peoples' = of peoples.

Try to avoid using **Lloyd's** (the insurance market) as a possessive; it poses an insoluble problem.

BRACKETS. If a whole sentence is within brackets, put the full stop inside.

Square brackets should be used for interpolations in direct quotations: **"Let them [the poor] eat cake."** To use ordinary curved brackets implies that the words inside them were part of the original text from which you are quoting.

COLONS. Use a colon "to deliver the goods that have been invoiced in the preceding words" (Fowler). **They brought presents: gold, frankincense and oil at $35 a barrel.**

Use a colon before a whole quoted sentence, but not before a quotation that begins mid-sentence. **She said: "It will never work." He retorted that it had "always worked before".**

Use a colon for antithesis or "gnomic contrasts" (Fowler). **Man proposes: God disposes.**

COMMAS. Use commas as an aid to understanding. Too many in one sentence can be confusing.

It is not necessary to put a comma after a short phrase at the start of a sentence if no natural pause exists there: **On August 2nd he invaded. Next time the world will be prepared.** But a breath, and so a comma, is needed after longer passages: **When it was plain that he had his eyes on Saudi Arabia as well as Kuwait, America responded.**

Use two commas, or none at all, when inserting a clause in the middle of a sentence. Thus, do not write: **Use two commas, or none at all when inserting ...** or **Use two commas or none at all, when inserting ...**

But, in 1968, students revolted; not **But in 1968, students revolted.**

If the clause ends with a bracket, which is not uncommon (this one does), the bracket should be followed by a comma.

Do not put a comma before **and** at the end of a sequence of items unless one of the items includes another **and**. Thus **The doctor suggested an aspirin, half a grapefruit and a cup of broth.** But **He ordered scrambled eggs, whisky and soda, and a selection from the trolley.** But American usage is different; see PART II, page 85.

Commas are useful to break up a long sentence, but should be used only where the break is a natural one. Do not insert or remove commas unnecessarily on proofs.

Commas in dates: none.

Do not put commas after question marks, even when they would be separated by quotation marks: **"Come into the garden, Maude?" he queried.**

DASHES. You can use dashes in pairs for parenthesis, but not more than one pair per sentence, ideally not more than one pair per paragraph. (See also HYPHENS.)

Use a dash to introduce an explanation, amplification, paraphrase, particularisation or correction of what immediately precedes it.

Use it to gather up the subject of a long sentence.

Use it to introduce a paradoxical or whimsical ending to sentences.

Do not use the dash as a punctuation maid-of-all-work (Gower).

FULL STOPS. Use plenty. They keep sentences short. This helps the reader.

Do not use full stops in ABBREVIATIONS or at the end of headings or rubrics.

INVERTED COMMAS (QUOTATION MARKS). Use single ones only for quotations within quotations. Thus: **"When I say 'immediately', I mean some time before April," said the spokesman.**

When a quotation is indented and set in smaller type than the main bodymatter, do not put inverted commas on it.

For the relative placing of quotation marks and punctuation, follow Hart's rules. If an extract ends with a full stop or question-mark, put the punctuation before the closing inverted commas. **"What's the difference between a buffalo and a bison?" she asked. The unhelpful answer was that "You can't wash your hands in a buffalo."** If a complete sentence in quotes comes at the end of a longer sentence, the final stop should be inside the inverted commas. Thus, **He said curtly "It cannot be done."**

If the quotation does not include any punctuation, the closing inverted commas should precede any punctuation marks that the sentence requires. An example from Hart: **"The passing crowd" is a phrase coined in the spirit of indifference. Yet, to a man of what Plato calls "universal sympathies", and even to the plain, ordinary denizens of this world, what can be more interesting than those who constitute "the passing crowd"?**

When a quotation is broken off and resumed after such words as **he said**, ask yourself whether it would naturally have had any punctuation at the point where it is broken off. If the answer is yes, a comma is placed within the quotation marks to represent this. Thus, **"It cannot be done," he said; "we must give up the task."** The comma after **done** belongs to the quotation and so comes within the inverted commas, as does the final full stop.

But if the words to be quoted are continuous, without punctuation at the point where they are broken, the comma should be outside the inverted commas. Thus, **"Go home", he said, "to your father."**

See PART II, pages 85–86, for American usage.

SEMI-COLONS. Semi-colons should be used to mark a pause longer than a comma and shorter than a full stop. Don't overdo them.

Use them to distinguish phrases listed after a colon if commas will not do the job clearly. Thus, **They agreed on only three points: the ceasefire should be immediate; it should be internationally supervised, preferably by the OAU; and a peace conference should be held, either in Geneva or in Ouagadougou.**

SQUARE BRACKETS. This form of parenthesis has a few limited, specific uses. Its main function is to indicate that the enclosed words have been added to the original text by someone other than the author. See also BRACKETS, HYPHENS.

QUOTATION MARKS. See INVERTED COMMAS.

R

RACISM. As a general rule, a person's race, colour or creed should be mentioned only when relevant. See ETHNIC GROUPS.

REAL. Is it really necessary? When used to mean **after taking inflation into account**, it is legitimate. In other contexts (**Investors are showing real interest in the country, but Bolivians wonder if real prosperity will ever arrive**), it is often better left out.

REASON. Because usually has no place in sentences involving the word **reason**. The reason is **that** it is redundant. **That** is the word. **That** should also be used after **reason** on many occasions when the temptation is to use **why**. The reason you think you should always write **the reason why** is your familiarity with the title *The Reason Why*. But that book takes its name from Tennyson's "Theirs not to reason why", where reason is being used as a verb.

REFUTE. If the law presumes you are innocent unless proved guilty, you can merely **deny** or **repudiate** an accusation; it is the prosecution's task to **refute** your claim, that is, to prove that your statement is false.

REGRETTABLY means it is to be regretted that; someone who shows regret is behaving **regretfully**. It is regrettably true that few people respond regretfully when told they have dropped some litter.

RELATIONSHIP is a long word often better replaced by **relations**. **The two countries hope for a better relationship** means **The two countries hope for better relations**.

RELATIVE: fine as an adjective, but as a noun prefer **relation**.

REPORT on, not **into**.

S

SAME: often superfluous. If your sentence contains **on the same day that**, try **on the day that**.

SCOTCH: to scotch means to **disable**, not to **destroy**. ("**We have scotched the snake, not killed it**"). The people may be Scots or Scottish (whisky is **Scotch**); choose as you like. **Scot-free** means **free from payment of a fine** (or **punishment**), not **free from Scotsmen**.

SCULPT: avoid. The verb, as well as the noun, is **sculpture**.

SECTOR: try **industry** instead.

SEXISM. It is often possible to phrase sentences so that they neither give offence to women nor become hideously complicated. Using the plural can be helpful. Thus **Instruct the reader without lecturing him** is better put as **Instruct the readers without lecturing them**. But some sentences cannot be satisfactorily rephrased in the plural: **The next president of the United States, whether he is a Democrat or a Republican, will have to get on with Congress.**

Since most alternatives to **man** words – such as **chairperson, humankind** and **person in the street** – are as ugly as the expression gender-neutral, they are best avoided. But remember that, in some contexts, the assumption that all people are men will be especially annoying just because it is wrong. **He will have to choose the best man for the job** is fine if you are talking about the pope selecting a bishop. If you are talking about John Major appointing a new member of cabinet, it would be better to say **He will have to choose the best person for the job**.

Do not use words that make unwarranted assumptions about the sex of an interest group. Do you mean **housewives** or **consumers, mothers** or **parents**?

Refer to **women**, not **girls** (unless they are under 18) or **ladies**. If more women read *The Economist*, there would be fewer jobs for the boys.

SHORT WORDS. Use them. They are often Anglo-Saxon rather than Latin in origin. They are easy to spell and easy to understand. Thus prefer **about** to **approximately**, **after** to **following**, **let** to **permit**, **but** to **however**, **use** to **utilise**, **make** to **manufacture**, **plant** to **facility**, **take part** to **participate**, **set up** to **establish**, enough to **sufficient, show** to **demonstrate,** and so on. **Under-developed** countries are often better described as **poor. Substantive** usually means **real** or **big.**

SIMPLISTIC: prefer **simple-minded, naive.**

SLANG. Do not be too free with **slang** (eg, **He really hit the big time in 1966**). Slang, like metaphors, should be used only occasionally if it is to have effect. Avoid expressions used only by journalists, such as giving people **the thumbs up, the thumbs down** or **the green light.** Stay clear of **gravy trains** and **salami tactics.** Do not use **the likes of.** And avoid words or expressions that are ugly or overused, such as **the bottom line, caring** (as an adjective), **carers, guesstimate** (use **guess**), **schizophrenic** (unless the context is medical), **crisis, key, major** (unless something else nearby is **minor**), **massive** (as in **massive inflation**), **meaningful, perceptions** and **prestigious.**

Politicians are often said to be highly **visible,** when **conspicuous** would be more appropriate. Regulations are sometimes said to be designed to create **transparency,** which presumably means they are intended to let people know **what is going on.**

Try not to be predictable, especially not predictably jocular. Spare your readers any mention of **mandarins** when writing about the civil service, of **their lordships** when discussing the House of Lords, and of **comrades** when analysing communist parties.

SMALL CAPITALS. Use SMALL CAPITALS for most abbreviations consisting of the first letter(s) of the abbreviated word(s). Exceptions are: currencies; degrees of temperature; some measures; Latin words. See also ABBREVIATIONS.

SOME TIME means **at some point; sometime** means **former.**

SPELLING

Use British English rather than American English or any other kind (see also PART II). Sometimes, however, this injunction will clash with the rule that people and companies should be called what they want to be called, short of festooning themselves with titles. If it does, adopt American (or Canadian or other local) spelling when it is used in the name of an American (etc) company or private organisation (**Alcan Aluminum, Pulverizing Services Inc, Travelers Insurance**), but not when it is used for a place or government institution (**Pearl Harbour, Department of Defence, Department of Labour**). The principle behind this ruling is that place names are habitually changed from foreign languages into English: **Deutsch-**

land becomes **Germany, München Munich, Torino Turin,** etc. And to respect the local spelling of government institutions would present difficulties: a sentence containing both the **Department of Labor** and the **secretary of labour,** or the **Defense Department** and the **need for a strong defence,** would look unduly odd. That oddity will arise nonetheless if you have to explain that **Rockefeller Center Properties is in charge of Rockefeller Centre,** but with luck that will not happen too often.

The Australian **Labor Party** should be spelt without a **u** not only because it is not a government institution but also because the Australians spell it that way, although they spell **labour** as the British do.

Use **-ise, -isation (realise, organisation)** throughout. But please do not **hospitalise.**

Follow the preferences of companies or individuals themselves in writing their names.

For spelling rules for place names, see CITIES; COUNTRIES AND THEIR INHABITANTS; NAMES; PLACES; STATES, REGIONS, PROVINCES, COUNTIES.

For spelling rules for other proper names, see PEOPLE and COMPANIES. Other common difficulties are listed below (and see also -ABLE, -EABLE, -IBLE. See also PART II for American spellings.

Common problems

accommodate
acknowledgment
adaptation (*not* adaption)
adviser, advisory
aeroplane, aircraft, airliner
aesthetic
affront
Afrikaans (the language),
  Afrikaner (the person)
ageing (*but* caging, paging,
  raging, waging)
all right (*not* alright)
almanac
ambience
amid (*not* amidst)
amok (*not* amuck)
annex (verb), annexe (noun)
aqueduct
aquifer
arbitrager
artefact
balk (*not* baulk)
bandwagon

battalion
benefited
biased
bicentenary (noun, *not*
  bicentennial)
block (*never* bloc)
blond (for either sex;
  blonde for females only)
bogey (bogie is on a locomotive)
born (given birth to),
  borne (carried)
burnt
bused, busing (keep bussing
  for kissing)
by-election, bypass, by-product
bye (in sport only)
bye-law (different root from
  by-election, etc)
callous (adj), callus (noun)
cannon (gun), canon (standard,
  criterion, clergyman)
canvas (cloth), canvass (seek
  opinion), canvassed

caviare

chancellor

channelled

chaperon

checking account (spell it thus
  when explaining to Americans
  a current account, which is
  to be preferred)

commemorate

commit (-ment)

complement (make complete),
  compliment (praise)

connection

consensus

coruscate

council (assembly)

councillor (*but* Privy Council,
  Privy Counsellor)

counsel (give advice)

counsellor

defendant

dependant (person)
  dependent (adj)

depository (*unless* referring to
  American depositary receipts)

desiccation

detente (*not* détente)

D-mark

dexterous (*not* dextrous)

discreet (prudent),
  discrete (separate)

disk (in a computer context),
  otherwise disc

dispatch (*not* despatch)

dispel, dispelling

dissect

dissociate (*not* disassociate)

distil, distiller

divergences

douse (drench),
  dowse (use a divining rod)

dreamed

dwelt

dyeing (colour)

dyke

ecstasy

embarrass (*but* harass)

encyclopedia

enroll, enrolment

ensure (make certain),
  insure (against risks)

farther (distance),
  further (additional)

ferreted

fetid

fetus (*not* foetus, misformed
  from the Latin *fetus*)

Filipino, Filipina (person),
  Philippine (adj of the
  Philippines)

filleted

flier, high-flier

flu (*not* 'flu)

focused, focusing

forbear (abstain),
  forebear (ancestor)

forbid (past tense forbade)

foreboding

foreclose

forefather

forestall

forewarn

forgather

forgo (do without),
  forego (precede)

forsake

forswear, forsworn

for ever (for all time),
  forever (unceasingly)

fuelled

-ful, *not* -full (armful,
  bathful, handful, etc)

fulfil, fulfilling

fullness

fulsome

gauge

gourmand

grey

grill (cook under flame)

grille (grating)

grisly (gruesome),
  grizzly (grey-haired;
  kind of bear)

guerrilla

gypsy
haemorrhage,
  haemorrhoids
hallo (*not* hello)
harass (*but* embarrass)
hiccup (*not* hiccough)
high-tech
hotch-potch
hurrah (*not* hooray)
hypocrisy, hypocrite
idiosyncrasy
idyll
imposter
in so far
incur, incurring
innocuous
inoculate
inquire, inquiry (*not* enquire,
  enquiry)
install, instalment, installation
instil, instilling
intransigent
jail (*not* gaol)
jewellery (*not* jewelry)
judgment
labelled
lacquer
laisser-faire
lama (priest), llama (beast)
learnt
leukaemia
levelled
liaise
libelled
licence (noun), license (verb)
lightening (making light),
  lightning (thunder and)
limited
linchpin, *but* lynch law
liqueur (flavoured alcoholic
  drink)
liquor (alcohol or other liquid)
literal (exact, factual, etc),
  littoral (shore)
loth (reluctant),
  loath (hate), loathsome
lour (frown), louring

low-tech
manoeuvre (manoeuvring)
mantelpiece
marshal (noun and verb)
marshalled
medieval
meter (instrument for
  measuring),
  metre (linear measurement)
mileage
millenary (of a thousand)
millennium (thousand years)
minuscule
modelled
mould
mouth (noun and verb)
mucous (adj), mucus (noun)
mujaheddin
Muslim (*not* Moslem)
naivety
'Ndragheta
nonplussed
nought (for numerals), *otherwise*
  naught
occur, occurring
paediatric (-ian)
parallel (-ed)
  paralleling
pastime
pedal (noun and verb,
  relating to foot lever)
peddle (to deal in trifles), *but*
  pedlar (*not* peddler)
peninsula (noun),
  peninsular (adj)
phoney (*not* phony)
phosphorus (noun, *not*
  phosphorous)
piggyback (pickaback)
Politburo
practice (noun), practise (verb)
predilection
preferred (-ing, *but* proffered)
primeval
principal (head; loan; or adj),
  principle (abstract noun)
privilege

proffered (-ing, *but* preferred)
profited
program (only in a computer
  context *otherwise* programme)
pronunciation
protester
pygmy
questionnaire
rankle
raze (*not* rase)
razzmattazz
recur, recurrent, recurring
refrigerator (*but* fridge)
regretted
renege
repairable (able to be repaired),
  reparable (of loss, able to be
  made good)
resemble, resemblance
restaurant
restaurateur
rottweiler
saccharin (noun),
  saccharine (adj)
sacrilegious
salutary (remedial),
  salutatory (welcoming)
sanatorium
savannah
sceptic
seize
shaky
sheath (noun), sheathe (verb)
siege
sieve
skulduggery
smelt
smidgen (*not* smidgeon)
smooth (both noun and verb)
soothe
soyabean
specialty (*only* in context of
  medicine, steel and chemicals),

otherwise speciality
spoilt
stationary (adj, not moving
  or movable)
stationery (noun, writing
  paper, etc)
storey (floor)
straight (without curves)
straits (narrow passage of water;
  position of difficulty)
stratagem
strategy
superseded
swap (*not* swop)
synonym
teetotalism, teetotaller
telephone (*not* phone)
television (*just occasionally* TV)
threshold
trade union, trade unions
  (*but* Trades Union Congress)
transatlantic (*unless* trans-Pacific
  occurs close to it, when it must
  be trans-Atlantic
transferred (-ing)
transsexual
travelled
tsar
unparalleled
vaccinate
vacillate
visor
wagon (*not* waggon)
waive (to relinquish rights)
waver (to vacillate, tremble)
whisky (Scotch), whiskey (Irish)
wilful
withhold
word processor
wreath (noun),
  wreathe (verb)
wry, wrily

SPLIT INFINITIVES. To never split an infinitive is quite easy.

-STYLE: avoid **German-style supervisory boards, a Yugoslav-style rotating prime minister,** etc. Explain what you mean.

SUBJUNCTIVES. See INTRODUCTION, pages 6–7; MAY AND MIGHT.

T

TABLE: avoid it as a transitive verb. In Britain to **table** means to bring something forward for action. In America it means the opposite.

TARGET is a noun. If you are tempted to use it as a verb, try **aim** or **direct**. **Targeted** means **provided with a shield.**

THERE IS, THERE ARE: often unnecessary. **There were smiles on every face** is better as **A smile was on every face. There are three issues facing the prime minister** is better as **Three issues face the prime minister.**

TIME. The time should always be given in figures with a stop between hours and minutes. Use the 12-hour clock and specify **am** and **pm** (with no stops and no space).

TIMES: take care. **Three times more than x** means **four times as much as x.**

TITLES.
The overriding principle is to treat people with respect. That usually means giving them the title they themselves adopt. But some titles are misleading (all Italian graduates are Dr), and some tiresomely long (Mr Dr Dr Federal Sanitary-Inspector Schmidt). Do not indulge people's self-importance unless it would seem insulting not to.

Do not use Mr, Mrs, Miss, Ms or Dr on first mention even in bodymatter. Plain George Bush, John Major or other appropriate combination of first name and surname will do. But thereafter the names of all living people should be preceded by Mr, Mrs, Ms, Miss or some other title. Knights, dames, lords, princes, kings, etc, should be given their title on first and subsequent mentions.

Titles are not necessary in headings or captions (surnames are; no Maggies, Georges, etc). Sometimes they can also be dispensed with for athletes and rock stars, if titles would make them seem more

ridiculous than dignified, and for criminals whose misdeeds are egregious. No titles for the dead, except those whom you are writing about because they have just died. **Dr Johnson** and **Mr Gladstone** are also permissible.

Take care with foreign titles. Malaysian ones are so confusing that it is wise to dispense with them altogether. Do not, however, call **Tunku Razaleigh Hamzah** Mr Razaleigh Hamzah; if you are not giving him his Tunku, refer to him, on each mention, as **Razaleigh Hamzah**. Avoid, above all, Mr Tunku Razaleigh Hamzah.

Use **Dr** only for qualified medical people, unless the correct alternative is not known or it would seem perverse to use **Mr**. And try to keep **Professor** for those who hold chairs, not just a university job or inflated ego.

If you use a title, get it right. **Rear-Admiral** Jones should not, at least on first mention, be called **Admiral** Jones.

Governor X, President Y, the Rev John Z may be **Mr, Mrs** or **Miss** on second mention.

Peeresses should be called **Lady**, not **Baroness**, just as barons are called **Lord**.

On first mention use forename and surname; thereafter drop forename (unless there are two people with the same surname mentioned in the article). **Neil Kinnock** then **Mr Kinnock**.

Avoid nicknames and diminutives unless the person is always known (or prefers to be known) by one: **Tony Benn, Dan Quayle, Tiny Rowland, Tip O'Neill, Dick Thornburgh**.

Avoid the habit of joining office and name: **Prime Minister Major, Environment Commissioner Ruffolo**, but **Chancellor Kohl** is permissible.

Omit middle initials. Nobody will imagine that the **Lyndon Johnson** you are writing about is **Lyndon A. Johnson** or **Lyndon C. Johnson**.

The title **Ms**, created to provide a female equivalent for the all-purpose male title **Mr**, is permissible though ugly. Married women who are known by their maiden names – eg, Aung San Suu Kyi, Benazir Bhutto, Jane Fonda – are **Miss** unless they have made it clear that they want to be called something else. Whenever possible, find out which title the woman herself prefers.

Some titles serve as names, and therefore have initial capitals, though they also serve as descriptions: **the Archbishop of Canterbury, the Emir of Sokoto**. If you want to describe the office rather than the individual, use lower case: **The next archbishop of Canterbury will be a woman**. Use lower case, too, in references simply to **the archbishop, the emir, the shah: The Duchess of Scunthorpe was in her finery, but the duke wore jeans**.

TOTAL: all right as a noun, but as a verb prefer **amount to** or **add up to**.

U

UNIQUE means **the only one of its kind** and cannot be qualified; it is nonsense to describe something or someone as **almost/rather/the most unique**.

UNLIKE should not be followed by **in**.

UNNECESSARY WORDS. Some words add nothing but length to your prose. Use adjectives to make your meaning more precise and be cautious of those you find yourself using to make it more emphatic. The word **very** is a case in point. If it occurs in a sentence you have written, try leaving it out and see whether the meaning is changed. **The omens were good** may have more force than **The omens were very good**.

Avoid **strike action** (**strike** will do), **cutbacks** (**cuts**), **track record** (**record**), **wilderness area** (usually either a **wilderness** or a **wild area**), **large-scale** (**big**), **weather conditions** (**weather**), etc.

Shoot off, or rather shoot, as many prepositions after verbs as possible. Thus people can **meet** rather than **meet together**; companies can be **bought** and **sold** rather than **bought up** and **sold off**; budgets can be **cut** rather than **cut back**; plots can be **hatched** but not **hatched up**; children can be **sent** to bed rather than **sent off** to bed.

The word **community** is usually unnecessary. So the **black community** means **blacks**, the **business community** means **business**, the **homosexual community** means **homosexuals**, the **international community**, if it means anything, means **other countries**, **aid agencies** or, just occasionally, **the family of nations**.

Use words with care. A **heart condition** is usually a **bad heart**. **Positive thoughts** (held by long-suffering creditors, according to *The Economist*) presumably means **optimism**. **Industrial action** is usually **industrial inaction**, **industrial disruption** or **strike**. A **substantially finished** bridge is an **unfinished** bridge, a **major speech** usually just a **speech**. Something with **reliability problems** probably **does not work**. If yours is a **live audience**, what would a dead one be like?

Also avoid KEY, LIFESTYLE, PROBLEM, SLANG, **global**, **ethnic**.

USE AND ABUSE: two words much used and abused. You **take** drugs, not **use** them (Does he use sugar?). And **drug abuse** is just **drug taking**, as is **substance abuse**, unless it is **glue sniffing** or **bun throwing**.

V • W

VENAL. In some countries, the majority of petty officials are **venal** – that is, open to bribery – but, when you consider what a paltry salary they are paid, you may count it a **venial** – that is, pardonable – sin.

VENERABLE means **worthy of reverence**. It is not a synonym for **old**.

VENUES: avoid them. Try **places**.

VERBAL: every agreement, except the nod-and-wink variety, is **verbal**. If you mean one that was not written down, describe it as **oral**.

VIABLE means **capable of living**. Do not apply it to things like railway lines. **Economically viable** means **profitable**.

•

WARN is transitive, so you must either **give warning** or **warn somebody**.

WHICH informs, **that** defines. **This is the house that Jack built.** But **This house, which Jack built, is now falling down.**

WHILE is best used temporally. Do not use it in place of **although** or **whereas**.

PART II

AMERICAN AND BRITISH ENGLISH

T he differences between English as written and spoken in America and English as used in Britain are considerable, as is the potential for misunderstanding, even offence, when using words or phrases that are unfamiliar or mean something else on the other side of the Atlantic. This section highlights the important differences of American and British English spelling, grammar and usage.

VOCABULARY. Sometimes the same word has taken on different meanings on the two sides of the Atlantic, creating an opportunity for misunderstanding. The word **homely**, for example, means **simple** or **informal** in British English, but **plain** or **unattractive** in American English.

This also applies to figures of speech. **It went like a bomb** in British English means it was a great success; **it bombed** in American English means it was a disaster. **To table** something in British English means to bring it forward for action; in American English it means the opposite.

EXCLUSIVITY. What is familiar in one culture may be entirely alien in another. British English exploits terms and phrases borrowed from the game of cricket; American English uses baseball terms. Anyone writing for readers in both markets uses either set of terms at their peril. Do not make references or assumptions that are geographically exclusive, for example by specifying months when referring to seasonal patterns, by using north or south to imply a type of climate, or by making geographical references that give state name followed by USA, as in Wyoming, USA.

One writer's slang is another's lively use of words; formal language to one is pomposity to another. This is the trickiest area to negotiate when writing for both British and American readers. At its best, distinctively American English is more direct and vivid than its British English equivalent. Many American words and expressions have passed into British English because they are shorter or more to the point: phrases like **lay off**, preferable to **make redundant**. But American English also has a contrary tendency to lengthen words, creating a (to British readers) pompous tone: words like **transportation** (in British English, **transport**), or **obligate** (**oblige**). One American ambassador to Britain discovered this after describing his first impressions of his new home as **necessitating a degree of refurbishment**.

British English is slower than American English to accept new words, and suspicious of short cuts. In particular, it resists the use as verbs of nouns such as **author, critique, host, impact, haemorrhage, loan, party, pressure** and **roundtable**; also **gun** (**down**) which means **shoot**. American English, however, does not like some perfectly good words – **sufficient** is almost always **enough** and **comprise** becomes **contain, include** or **is made up of**. American English is also fast to adopt new usages for words such as **scenario, posture, parameter**.

SYNTAX AND SENTENCE STRUCTURE. American English may also use different syntax and sentence construction. Written American English tends to be more declarative than its British counterpart, and adverbs and some modifying phrases are frequently positioned differently. For example, British English may say, "**As well as going shopping, we went to the park.**" American English would turn the opening phrase around: "**We went to the park as well as going shopping**", or would begin the sentence with "**In addition to**". British English also tends to use more compound modifying phrases, while American English prefers to go with simpler sentence structure.

In British English doctors and lawyers are to be found **in** Harley Street or Wall Street, not **on** it. And they rest from their labours **at** weekends, not **on** them. During the week their children are **at** school, not **in** it.

Words may also be inserted or omitted in some standard phrases. British English goes **to hospital**, American English **to the hospital**. British English may **stop a child running into the road**, while American English would **stop it from running in the road**. British English chooses between **one or other thing**; American English chooses **one thing or the other**.

SPELLING. Some words are spelt differently; the spellings are sufficiently similar to identify the word, but the unfamiliar form may still disturb the reader. It may be better to use a synonym than to take this risk, although sometimes it cannot be avoided.

SPECIAL PROBLEMS. A number of subjects call for highly detailed, specialised guidance beyond the scope of this book, though some of the vocabulary is dealt with here. These areas include food and cookery (different names for ingredients and equipment; different systems of measurement); medicine and health care (different professional titles, drug names, therapies); human anatomy (different attitudes to the depiction of sexual organs); and gardening (different seasons and plants). Many crafts and hobbies also use different terms for equipment, materials and techniques.

–ISMS. The difficulties that arise in Europe with references to race and sex (see ETHNIC GROUPS, SEXISM) are even greater in America where readers are often more sensitive. It is currently difficult to advise how to refer to Americans whose ancestors came from Africa; preferred usage appears to be no longer **black** but there is no agreed alternative. It is totally unacceptable to refer to **American Indians** as **red**. It can also cause offence to describe the original inhabitants of the lands stretching from Greenland to Alaska as **Eskimos**; this was a corruption of a Cree word meaning **raw flesh eater**. The people themselves have at least three major tribal groupings. **Alaska native** is relatively acceptable (if in Alaska) and so is **Inuit**, though as this means men it may not last.

It is unwise to describe an adult American female as a **girl**.

A JOINT DICTIONARY

USE -IZE, NOT -ISE. The American convention is to spell with **z** many words that the British spell with **s**. Few British readers object to this. Remember, though, that some words must end in **-ise**, whichever spelling convention is being followed. These include:

advertise	despise	incise
advise	devise	merchandise
apprise	disguise	premise
arise	emprise	prise
chastise	enfranchise	revise
circumcise	excise	supervise
comprise	exercise	surmise
compromise	franchise	surprise
demise	improvise	televise

Note that words with the ending **-lyse**, such as **analyse** and **paralyse**, should not be spelt **-lyze** in British English, even though they are commonly spelt thus in American English.

WORDS GENERALLY ACCEPTABLE IN BOTH BRITISH AND AMERICAN ENGLISH

ambience *not* ambiance
among *not* amongst
annex *not* annexe
artifact *not* artefact
backward *not* backwards
baptistry *not* baptistery
Bible *not* bible
Bordeaux *not* claret, for red wine of region
burned *not* burnt
bus *not* coach
busy *not* engaged, for telephones
canvases *not* canvasses

car rental *not* car hire
carryall *not* holdall
cater to *not* cater for
custom-made *not* bespoke
day nursery *not* crèche
development *not* estate, for housing
diesel fuel *not* derv
disc *not* disk, except in computing
dispatch *not* despatch
encyclopedia *not* encyclopaedia
except for *not* save

farther *not* further, for distance
first name *not* Christian name
flashlight *not* torch
flip *not* toss, for coin, etc
floor *not* storey (UK) or story (US)
focusing, focused, etc
fuel *not* petrol (UK) or gasoline (US)
forward *not* forwards
(eye)glasses *not* spectacles
grille *not* grill, for grating
gypsy *not* gipsy
hairdryer *not* hairdrier
horse-racing *not just* racing
inquire *not* enquire
insurance coverage *not* insurance cover
intermission *not* interval
jail *not* gaol
learned *not* learnt
like *not* fancy
line *not* queue
located *not* situated
location *not* situation
mathematics *not* maths (UK) or math (US)
merry-go-round *not* roundabout
motorcycle *not* motorbike
neat *not* spruce or tidy
newsstand *not* kiosk
nightgown *not* nightdress
okra *not* lady's fingers
onto *not* on to
orangeade/lemonade *not* orange/lemon squash
package *not* parcel
parking spaces/garage *not* car park (UK) or parking lot (US)
pharmacy *not* chemist (UK) or drugstore (US)
phoney *not* phony
priority *not* right of way, for vehicles

refrigerator *not* fridge
rail station *not* railway station (UK) or railroad station (US)
raincoat *not* mac, mackintosh
rent *not* hire, except for people
reservation, reserve (seats, etc) *not* booking, book
retired person *not* old-age pensioner (UK) or retiree (US)
room maid *not* chambermaid
sanatorium *not* sanitarium
slowdown *not* go-slow, in production
soccer *not* football, except for American football
sorbet *not* water-ice (UK) or sherbet (US)
spelled *not* spelt
spoiled *not* spoilt
street musician *not* busker
swap *not* swop
swimming *not* bathing
team *not* side, in sport
tearoom *not* teashop
thread *not* cotton
toilet *not* lavatory
toll-free *not* free of charge
trainers *not* plimsolls (UK) or sneakers (US)
trousers *not* pants
tuna *not* tunny
underwear *not* pants or knickers; or use lingerie for women's underwear
unmistakable *not* unmistakeable
unspoiled *not* unspoilt
while *not* whilst
whimsy, whimsies *not* whimsey, whimseys
workman *not* navvy
yogurt *not* yoghourt or yoghurt

PROBLEMATIC WORDS AND PHRASES

DIFFERENT SPELLING CONVENTIONS.

American English is more obviously phonetic than British English. The word **cosy** becomes **cozy**, **aesthetic** becomes **esthetic**, **sizeable** becomes **sizable**, **arbour** becomes **arbor**, **theatre** becomes **theater**, **draught** becomes **draft**.

The main spelling differences between American English and British English are as follows.

-eable/-able. The silent e, created when forming some adjectives with this suffix, is more often omitted in American English; thus, **likeable** is spelt **likable**, **unshakeable** is spelt **unshakable**. But the e is sometimes retained in American English where it affects the sound of the preceding consonant; thus, **traceable**, or **manageable**.

-ae/-oe. Although it is now common in British English to write **medieval** rather than **mediaeval**, other words – often scientific terms such as **aeon**, **diarrhoea**, **aesthetic**, **gynaecology**, **homoeopathy** – retain their classical composite vowel. In American English, the composite vowel is replaced by a single e; thus, **eon**, **diarrhea**, **esthetic**, **gynecology**, **homeopathy**.

-ce/-se. In British English, the verb that relates to a noun ending in -ce is sometimes given the ending -se; thus, **advice** (noun), **advise** (verb), **device/devise**, **licence/license**, **practice/practise**. In the first two instances, the spelling change is accompanied by a slight change in the sound of the word; but in the other two instances, noun and verb are pronounced the same way, and American English spelling reflects this, by using the same spelling: thus, **license and practice**. It also extends the use of -se to other nouns which in British English are spelt -ce: thus, **defense**, **offense**, **pretense**.

-e/-ue. The final silent e or ue of several words is omitted in American English but retained in British English: thus, **analog/ analogue**, **ax/axe**, **catalog/catalogue**.

-ll/-l. In British English, when words ending in the consonant l are given a suffix beginning with a vowel (eg, the suffixes -able, -ed, -ing, -ous, -y), the l is doubled; thus, **annul/annulled**, **model/modelling**, **quarrel/quarrelling**, **rebel/rebellious**, **wool/woolly**. This is inconsistent with the general rule in British English that the final consonant is doubled before the suffix only when the preceding vowel carries the main stress: thus, the word **regret** becomes **regretted**, or **regrettable**; but the word **billet** becomes **billeted**. American English mostly does not have this inconsistency. So if the stress does not fall on the preceding vowel, the l is not doubled: thus, model/modeling, travel/traveler; but **annul/annulled**.

Several words which end in a single l in British English – eg, **appal, fulfil** – take a double ll in American English. In British English, the l stays single when the word takes a suffix beginning with a consonant (eg, the suffixes -ful, -fully, -ment): thus, **fulfil/ fulfilment**. Moreover, words ending in -ll usually lose one l when taking one of these suffixes: thus, **skill/skilful, will/wilfully**. In American English, words ending in -ll usually remain intact, whatever the suffix: thus, **skill/skillful, will/willfully**.

-our/-or. Most British English words ending in -our – **ardour, behaviour, candour, demeanour, favour, valour** and the like – lose the u in American English: thus, **ardor, candor**, etc. The major exception is **glamour**, which retains its u.

-re/-er. Most British English words ending in -re – such as **centre, fibre, metre, theatre** – end in -er in American English: thus, **center, fiber**, etc. The exceptions include: **acre, cadre, lucre, massacre, mediocre, ogre**.

-t/-ed (past tense). British English uses -t – **spelt, learnt, burnt** – whereas American English uses -ed – **spelled, learned, burned**.

HYPHENATION.

American English is far readier than British English to accept compound words. In particular, many nouns made of two separate nouns are spelt as one word in American English, while in British English they would either remain separate or be joined by a hyphen: eg, **applesauce** (hyphenated in British English). British English also tends, more than American English, to use hyphens as pronunciation aids or to separate identical letters in words such as **co-operation, pre-empt, re-examine**.

American English likes hyphenated adjectives such as **in-depth, in-flight**, which although common in British English are deprecated.

COMMON PROBLEMATIC WORDS.

The following list draws attention to commonly used words and idioms that either are spelt differently or have different meanings in American English and British English. It does not cover slang or colloquialisms.

If you want to produce a single version of written material acceptable to both sorts of readers, you should avoid using the words in this list when there is a mutually acceptable alternative (see pages 76–77). If not, follow one or other convention, and, if this means using a word that will mystify or mislead one group of readers, provide a translation.

British	American
accommodation (lodging/s)	accommodation/s (lodging/s)
adopt (a candidate)	nominate
aerial (TV)	antenna
air hostess	flight attendant
aluminium	aluminum
anti-clockwise	counterclockwise
apophthegm	apothegm
apple purée	applesauce
at weekends	on weekends
aubergine	eggplant
autumn	fall
baby's dummy	pacifier
baking tray	baking sheet
bag, handbag	purse, pocketbook
banknote	bill
barrister	trial lawyer
behind	in back of
behove	behoove
bicarbonate of soda	baking soda
bilberry	blueberry
bill	check
biscuit (sweet)	cookie
biscuit (savoury)	cracker
black treacle	molasses
blind (for windows)	shade
bowler (hat)	derby
braces	suspenders
building society	savings and loan association
calibre	caliber
camp bed	cot
car, estate	station wagon
car, saloon	sedan
car accelerator	gas pedal
car bonnet	hood
car boot	trunk
car demister	defogger
car dipswitch	dimmer
car jump leads	jumper cables
car park	parking lot
car silencer	muffler
car windscreen	windshield
car wing	fender
caravan	house trailer
cheque (bank)	check
chequered	checkered (pattern)

British	American
chicken leg	drumstick
chickpea	garbanzo bean
chilli/chillies	chili/chilis
chips	French fries
choux bun	cream puff
cinema	movie theater
clarinettist	clarinetist
clever	smart
cling film	plastic wrap
coach	bus
coriander (fresh)	cilantro
corn	wheat
cornflour	cornstarch
cosy	cozy
cot	crib
country	nation
courgette	zucchini
crayfish	crawfish
crisps	chips
crossroads/junction	intersection
crystallized	candied
cupboard/wardrobe	closet
demerara sugar	light-brown sugar
desiccated coconut	shredded coconut
dialled	dialed
digestive biscuit	graham cracker
district	neighborhood
doctor	physician
double cream	heavy cream
draught	draft
dressing gown	bathrobe/housecoat
drug	narcotic
dual carriageway	four-lane (or divided) highway
dyke	dike
essence (eg, vanilla)	extract or flavoring
estate agent	realtor/real estate agent
ex-serviceman	veteran
eyrie	aerie
felafel	falafel
flan tin	pie pan
fillet (boneless meat/fish)	filet
flour, plain	flour, all-purpose
flour, self-raising	flour, self-rising
flour, wholemeal	flour, whole-wheat
flyover	overpass
from ... to ...	through

British	American
frying pan	skillet
fuelled	fueled
full stop (punctuation)	period
furore	furor
give way	yield
golden syrup	corn syrup
greengrocer's	vegetable market
grey	gray
grill (verb and noun)	broil (verb), broiler (noun)
ground floor	first floor
high street	main street
hire (of car)	rent
holiday	vacation (*but* public holiday)
home from home	home away from home
homely	homey/homy (homely = plain)
icing sugar	powdered or confectioners' sugar
in (Fifth Avenue, etc)	on
increase	hike
jeweller/jewellery	jeweler/jewelry
jumper	sweater
keep a promise	deliver (on a promise)
kerb/kerbside	curb/curbside
ketchup	catsup
labelled	labeled
ladder (in stocking)	run
lawyer	attorney
lease of life	lease on life
lift	elevator
liquidiser	blender
lorry	truck
lustre	luster
maize/sweetcorn	corn
manoeuvre/manoeuvrable	maneuver/maneuverable
marvellous	marvelous
mean (parsimonious)	stingy, tight (mean = nasty)
meet	meet with
metre (unit of distance)	meter
minced meat	ground meat
modelled	modeled
motor-racing	auto-racing
motorway	superhighway, freeway, expressway
mould/moulder/moult	mold/molder/molt
moustache	mustache
mum/mummy	mom/mommy
muslin	cheesecloth

British	*American*
nappy	diaper
nervy	nervous (nervy = brazen)
nominate, predict	slate
oblige	obligate
omelette	omelet
ordinary	regular, normal
outside	outside of
paddling pool	wading pool
panelled	wood-paneled
pants	underpants
pastry case	pie shell
pavement	sidewalk
pepper (red, green, etc)	capsicum or sweet pepper
petrol	gasoline, gas
petrol station	gas/service station
pips	seeds (in fruit)
pitta bread	pita bread
plain/dark chocolate	semisweet or unsweetened chocolate
plait	braid
plough	plow
podgy	pudgy
polythene	polyethylene
post, post box	mail, mailbox
power point	electrical outlet
pram, push chair	stroller
press stud	snap fastener
programme (except computer)	program
property (land)	real estate
pumpkin	squash
pyjamas	pajamas
quitted (past tense and participle of quit)	quit
rambler	hiker
removal van	moving van
request stop	flag stop
rationalisation	downsizing
riding (horses)	horseback riding
ring road	beltway
rivalled	rivaled
rowing boat	rowboat
run in (car, engine)	break in
scallywag	scalawag
sceptical	skeptical
senior	ranking (sometimes)
shortcrust pastry	pie dough

British	*American*
shorthand typist	stenographer
single cream	light cream
sizeable	sizable
skilful	skillful
sleepers	railroad ties
smoulder	smolder
soda water	seltzer
solicitor	attorney
sombre	somber
soya	soy
spanner	wrench
specialist shop	specialty shop
speciality (*but* specialty for medicine, steel and chemicals)	specialty
sponge finger biscuits	ladyfingers
spring onion	scallion
stand (for election)	run
stocks	inventory
stone	rock
stoned (cherries, etc)	pitted
storey (of building)	story
stupid	dumb
subway	pedestrian underpass
sulphur(ous)	sulfur(ous)
sultana	golden (seedless) raisin
suspenders	garters
sweated (past tense and participle of sweat)	sweat
sweet shop	candy store
tap	faucet
terraced house	row house
till	check-out
titbit	tidbit
tomato purée	tomato paste
towards	toward
transport	transportation
traveller/travelled	traveler/traveled
trousers	pants or slacks
trunk call	long-distance call
turning (road)	turnoff
tyre	tire
underground (or tube train)	subway
vest	undershirt
vice (tool)	vise
waistcoat	vest

British	American
walk	hike
water biscuit	cracker
way out	exit
woollen/woolly	woolen/wooly
work out (problem)	figure out
zip	zipper

DIFFERENCES IN PUNCTUATION

COMMA IN LISTS. American English puts a comma before the **and**. Thus in American English, **eggs, bacon, potatoes, and cheese**; in British English **eggs, bacon, potatoes and cheese**.

DASHES. In British publications, the usual style for a dash used as a parenthesis is an en-rule (–) with a character space either side. In American publications, the usual style for a dash is an em-rule (—) with no spaces.

FULL STOPS (PERIOD). The American convention is to use full stops (periods) to identify almost all abbreviations. The British convention is to keep them to a minimum.

QUOTATION MARKS. In American publications (and those of major Commonwealth countries), the convention is to use double quotation marks, reserving single quotation marks for quotes within quotes. In British publications, the convention is the reverse (except in *The Economist*): single quotation marks are used first, then double. However, the American style is becoming more popular.

The relative position of quotation marks and other punctuation is far more contentious. The British convention is to place such punctuation according to sense. The American convention is simpler but less logical: all commas and full stops precede the final quotation mark (or, if there is a quote within a quote, the first final quotation mark). Other punctuation – colons, semi-colons, question and exclamation marks – is placed according to sense. The following examples illustrate the differences.

American style

The words on the magazine's cover, "The link between coffee and cholesterol," caught his eye.

"You're eating too much," she told him. "You'll soon look like your father."

"Have you seen this article, 'The link between coffee and cholesterol'?" he asked.

"It was as if," he explained, "I had swallowed a toad, and it kept croaking 'ribbut, ribbut,' from deep in my stomach."

She particularly enjoyed the article "Looking for the 'New Man.' "

British style

The words on the magazine's cover, 'The link between coffee and cholesterol', caught his eye.

'You're eating too much,' she told him. 'You'll soon look like your father.'

'Have you seen this article, "The link between coffee and cholesterol"?' he asked.

'It was as if,' he explained, 'I had swallowed a toad, and it kept croaking "ribbut, ribbut", from deep in my belly.'

She particularly enjoyed the article 'Looking for the "New Man" '.

DIFFERENT UNITS OF MEASUREMENT

In British publications measurements are now largely expressed in SI units (the modern form of metric units), although imperial measures are still used in certain contexts. In American publications measurements may be expressed in SI or imperial units.

Although in most cases the British imperial and American standard measures are identical, there are some important exceptions. There are also some measures peculiar to one or other national system, particularly units of mass relating to agriculture. See also MEASUREMENTS (Part I) and MEASURES (Part III).

PART III

FACT CHECKER
AND
GLOSSARY

A

ABBREVIATIONS.

Here is a list of some common business abbreviations. (See also ABBREVIATIONS, pages 10–11.)

ACA	Associate of the Institute of Chartered Accountants in England and Wales, or Ireland
ACT	advance corporation tax (UK)
AG	Aktiengesellschaft (German or Swiss public limited company)
AGM	annual general meeting
APR	annual percentage rate
ASSC	Accounting Standards Steering Committee (UK)
CA	member of the Institute of Chartered Accountants of Scotland
CAPM	capital asset pricing model
CCA	current cost accounting
CGT	capital gains tax
cif	cost, insurance, freight
COB	Commission des Opérations de Bourse (Stock Exchange Commission, France)
Consob	Commissione Nazionale per le Società e la Borsa (Stock Exchange Commission, Italy)
CPA	certified public accountant (USA); critical path analysis
CPP	current purchasing power (accounting)
CTT	capital transfer tax
DCF	discounted cash flow
EC	European Community
ECU	European currency unit
EEC	European Economic Community
EFT	electronic funds transfer
EFTPOS	electronic funds transfer at point of sale
EMS	European Monetary System
EMU	economic and monetary union
EPS	earnings per share
ERM	exchange-rate mechanism
FASB	Financial Accounting Standards Board (USA)
FCA	Fellow of the Institute of Chartered Accountants in England and Wales, or Ireland
fob	free on board
GAAP	generally accepted accounting principles (USA)
GmbH	Gesellschaft mit beschränkter Haftung (German or Swiss

private limited company)

IRR	internal rate of return
IRS	Internal Revenue Service (USA)
LIFFE	London International Financial Futures Exchange
MCT	mainstream corporation tax
MLR	minimum lending rate
NASDAQ	National Association of Securities Dealers Automated Quotations System (USA)
NPV	net present value; no par value
NRV	net realisable value
P/E	price/earnings ratio
P&L a/c	profit and loss account
PLC	public limited company (UK)
PRT	petroleum revenue tax (UK)
PSBR	public-sector borrowing rate
R&D	research and development
ROCE	return on capital employed
ROI	return on investment
SA	société anonyme (French, Belgian, Luxembourg or Swiss public limited company)
SàrL	société à responsabilité limitée (French, etc private limited company)
SEAQ	Stock Exchange Automated Quotation System (UK)
SEC	Securities and Exchange Commission (USA)
SERPS	state earnings-related pension scheme
SRO	self-regulating organisation
SSAP	Statement of Standard Accounting Practice (UK)
UEC	Union Européenne des Experts Comptables Economiques et Financiers
USM	Unlisted Securities Market (UK)
VAT	value-added tax
ZBB	zero base budgeting

For international bodies and their abbreviations, see ORGANISATIONS (pages 124ff).

ACCENTS. Here are some of the more familiar foreign language accents.

acute	république
grave	grand'mère
circumflex	bête noire
umlaut	länder, Österreich (Austria)
cedilla	français
tilde	señor, São Paulo

ACCOUNTANCY RATIOS.

These are the ratios most commonly used in accounting practice.

Working capital

Working capital ratio = current assets/current liabilities, where current assets = stock + debtors + cash at bank and in hand + quoted investments, etc, current liabilities = creditors + overdraft at bank + taxation + dividends, etc. The ratio varies according to type of trade and conditions; a ratio from 1 to 3 is usual with a ratio above 2 being generally good.

Liquidity ratio = liquid ("quick") assets/current liabilities, where liquid assets = debtors + cash at bank and in hand + quoted investments (that is assets which can be realised within a month or so, which may not apply to all investments); current liabilities are those which may need to be repaid within the same short period, which may not necessarily include a bank overdraft where it is likely to be renewed. The liquidity ratio is sometimes referred to as the "acid test"; a ratio under 1 suggests a possibly difficult situation, while too high a ratio may mean that assets are not being usefully employed.

Turnover of working capital = sales/average working capital. The ratio varies according to type of trade; generally a low ratio can mean poor use of resources, while too high a ratio can mean over-trading.

Turnover of stock = sales/average stock, or (where cost of sales is known) = cost of sales/average stock. The cost of sales turnover figure is to be preferred as both figures are then on the same valuation basis. This ratio can be expressed as number of times per year, or time taken for stock to be turned over once = (52/number of times) weeks. A low turnover of stock can be a sign of stocks which are difficult to move, and is usually a sign of adverse conditions.

Turnover of debtors = credit sales/average debtors. This indicates efficiency in collecting accounts. An average "credit period" of about one month is usual, but varies according to credit stringency conditions in the economy.

Turnover of creditors = purchases/average creditors. Average payment period is best maintained in line with turnover of debtors.

Sales

Export ratio = exports as a percentage of sales.
Sales per employee = sales/average number of employees.

Assets

Ratios of assets can vary according to the measure of assets used:
Total assets = current assets + fixed assets + other assets, where fixed assets = property + plant and machinery + motor vehicles, etc, and other assets = long-term investment + goodwill, etc.
Net assets ("net worth") = total assets - total liabilities
= share capital + reserves

Turnover of net assets = sales/average net assets. As for turnover of working capital, a low ratio can mean poor use of resources.

Assets per employee = assets/average number of employees. Indicates the amount of investment backing for employees.

Profits

Profit margin = (profit/sales) x 100 = profits as a percentage of sales; usually profits before tax.

Profitability = (profit/total assets) x 100 = profits as a percentage of total assets.

Return on capital = (profit/net assets) x 100 = profits as a percentage of net assets ("net worth" or "capital employed").

B

BEAUFORT SCALE. The Beaufort Scale, once a picturesque fleet of well-scrubbed men-o'-war and fishing smacks, has been rendered bland by the World Meteorological Organization.

The Beaufort Scale

Conditions (abbreviated)

Force	Description	On land	At sea	Equivalent speed at 10m height		
				knots	miles per hour	metres per second
0	Calm	Smoke rises vertically	Sea like a mirror	less than 1	less than 1	0.0–0.2
1	Light air	Smoke drifts	Ripples	1–3	1–3	0.3–1.5
2	Light breeze	Leaves rustle	Small wavelets	4–6	4–7	1.7–3.3
3	Gentle breeze	Wind extends light flag	Large wavelets, crests break	7–10	8–12	3.4–5.4
4	Moderate breeze	Raises paper and dust	Small waves, some white horses	11–16	13–18	5.5–7.9
5	Fresh breeze	Small trees in leaf sway	Moderate waves, many white horses	17–21	19–24	8.0–10.7
6	Strong breeze	Large branches in motion	Large waves form, some spray	22–27	25–31	10.8–13.8
7	Moderate gale or near gale	Whole trees in motion	Sea heaps up, white foam streaks	28–33	32–38	13.9–17.1
8	Fresh gale or gale	Breaks twigs off trees	Moderately high waves, well-marked foam streaks	34–40	39–46	17.2–20.7
9	Strong gale	Slight structural damage to tumble over	High waves, crests start	41–47	47–54	20.8–24.4
10	Whole gale or storm	Trees uprooted, considerable structural damage	Very high waves, white sea tumbles	48–55	55–63	24.5–28.4
11	Storm or violent storm	Very rarely experienced, widespread damage	Exceptionally high waves, edges of wave crests blown to froth	56–63	64–72	28.5–32.6
12–17	Hurricane	Devastation with driving spray	Sea completely white	64–118	73–136	32.7–over

C

CALENDARS.

There are six important solar calendars.

Gregorian	Iranian[b]	Hindu[c]
January (31)[a]		
February (28 or 29)		
March (31)	Favardin (31)	Caitra (30)
April (30)	Ordibehesht (31)	Vaisakha (31)
May (31)	Khordad (31)	Jyaistha (31)
June (30)	Tir (31)	Asadha (31)
July (31)	Mordad (31)	Sravana (31)
August (31)	Sharivar (31)	Bhadrapada (31)
September (30)	Mehr (30)	Asvina (30)
October (31)	Aban (30)	Karttika (30)
November (30)	Azar (30)	Margasirsa (30)
December (31)	Dey (30)	Pausa (30)
(January)	Bahman (30)	Magha (30)
(February)	Esfand (28 or 29)	Phalguna (30)

Gregorian	Ethiopian[d]	Jewish[e]
September (30)	Maskerem (30)	Tishri (30)
October (31)	Tikimit (30)	Cheshvan (29 or 30)
November (30)	Hidar (30)	Kislev (29 or 30)
December (31)	Tahsas (30)	Tebet (29)
(January)	Tir (30)	Shebat (30)
(February)	Yekatit (30)	Adar (29)
(March)	Megabit (30)	Nisan (30)
(April)	Miazia (30)	Iyyar (29)
(May)	Guenbot (30)	Sivan (30)
(June)	Sene (30)	Tammuz (29)
(July)	Hamle (30)	Ab (30)
(August)	Nahassie (30+5 or 6)	Elul (29)

[a] Figures in brackets denote the number of days in that month.
[b] Months begin about the 21st of the corresponding Gregorian month.
[c] Months begin about the 22nd of the corresponding Gregorian month.
[d] Months begin on the 11th of the corresponding Gregorian month.
[e] The date of the new year varies, but normally falls in the second half of September in the Gregorian calendar; the general calendar position is maintained by adding, in some years, an extra period of 29 days, Adar Sheni, following the month of Adar.

The Muslim calendar. Muslims use a lunar calendar which begins 10 or 11 days earlier each year in terms of the Gregorian. The months do not, however, have a fixed number of days. The priesthood declares the official start of each month. The names of the months are as follows.

Muharram	Rajab
Safar	Shaaban
Rabia I	Ramadan
Rabia II	Shawwal
Jumada I	Dhu al-Kadah
Jumada II	Dhu al-Hijjah

In each 30 years, 19 years have 354 days (are "common") and 11 have 355 days (are "intercalary").

Muslim years begin on the following dates of the Gregorian calendar. The dates for 1993–96 are approximate.

1411	July 24th 1990
1412	July 13th 1991
1413	July 2nd 1992
1414	June 20th 1993
1415	June 9th 1994
1416	May 30th 1995
1417	May 18th 1996

CARS.

Here is a list of some international vehicle registration (IVR) letters.

A	Austria	F	France
AUS	Australia	GB	Great Britain
B	Belgium	GR	Greece
BD	Bangladesh	H	Hungary
BR	Brazil	HK	Hong Kong
CAM	Cameroon	I	Italy
CDN	Canada	IL	Israel
CH	Switzerland	IND	India
CI	Côte d'Ivoire	IR	Iran
CO	Colombia	IRL	Ireland
CS	Czechoslovakia	IRQ	Iraq
D	Germany	J	Japan
DK	Denmark	MA	Morocco
DZ	Algeria	MAL	Malaysia
E	Spain	MEX	Mexico
EAK	Kenya	N	Norway
ET	Egypt	NL	Netherlands

NZ	New Zealand		
P	Portugal	SF	Finland
PAK	Pakistan	SGP	Singapore
PE	Peru	SU	Soviet Union
PI	Philippines	T	Thailand
PL	Poland	USA	United States of
RA	Argentina		America
RC	Taiwan	WAN	Nigeria
RCH	Chile	YU	Yugoslavia
RI	Indonesia	YV	Venezuela
ROK	South Korea	ZA	South Africa
S	Sweden	ZRE	Zaire
SA	Saudi Arabia	ZW	Zimbabwe

CITIES. Correct spellings of the cities of the world with populations of more than 2m are listed here. These may be conurbations rather than metropolitan areas. Cities marked [a] are capital cities.

1	Mexico City[a]	*Mexico*	31	Santiago[a]	*Chile*
2	New York	*USA*	32	Leningrad	*Soviet Union*
3	Los Angeles	*USA*	33	Dacca[a]	*Bangladesh*
4	Cairo[a]	*Egypt*	34	Detroit	*USA*
5	Shanghai	*China*	35	Shenyang	*China*
6	Beijing[a] (Peking)	*China*	36	Madras	*India*
7	Seoul[a]	*South Korea*	37	Boston	*USA*
8	Calcutta	*India*	38	Bogotá[a]	*Colombia*
9	Moscow[a]	*Soviet Union*	39	Ho Chi Minh City	
10	Paris[a]	*France*		(Saigon)	*Vietnam*
11	São Paulo	*Brazil*	40	Dallas	*USA*
12	Tokyo[a]	*Japan*	41	Wuhan	*China*
13	Tianjin	*China*	42	Houston	*USA*
14	Bombay	*India*	43	Washington[a]	*USA*
15	Chicago	*USA*	44	Sydney	*Australia*
16	London[a]	*UK*	45	Pusan	*South Korea*
17	Jakarta[a]	*Indonesia*	46	Toronto	*Canada*
18	Lagos[a]	*Nigeria*	47	Ankara[a]	*Turkey*
19	San Francisco	*USA*	48	Canton (Guangzhou)	*China*
20	Manila[a]	*Philippines*	49	Caracas[a]	*Venezuela*
21	Philadelphia	*USA*	50	Yokohama	*Japan*
22	Istanbul	*Turkey*	51	Hanoi	*Vietnam*
23	Tehrana	*Iran*	52	Guadalajara	*Mexico*
24	Hong Kong[a]	*Hong Kong*	53	Athens[a]	*Greece*
25	Delhi[a]	*India*	54	Madrid[a]	*Spain*
26	Lima[a]	*Peru*	55	Melbourne	*Australia*
27	Baghdad[a]	*Iraq*	56	Montreal	*Canada*
28	Río de Janeiro	*Brazil*	57	Buenos Aires[a]	*Argentina*
29	Bangkok[a]	*Thailand*	58	Lahore	*Pakistan*
30	Karachi	*Pakistan*	59	Bangalore	*India*

60	Rome[a]	*Italy*	75	Aleppo	*Syria*
61	Chongqing	*China*	76	Xi'an	*China*
62	Alexandria	*Egypt*	77	Nanjing	*China*
63	Kinshasa[a]	*Zaire*	78	Santo Domingo[a]	
64	Casablanca	*Morocco*			*Dominican Republic*
65	Osaka	*Japan*	79	Ahmadabad	*India*
66	Monterrey	*Mexico*	80	Nagoya	*Japan*
67	Rangoon[a]	*Myanmar*	81	Tashkent	*Soviet Union*
68	Taipei[a]	*Taiwan*	82	Budapest[a]	*Hungary*
69	Harbin	*China*	83	Havana[a]	*Cuba*
70	Chengdu	*China*	84	Taegu	*South Korea*
71	Kiev	*Soviet Union*	85	Surabaya	*Indonesia*
72	Hyderabad	*India*	86	Pyongyang	*North Korea*
73	Singapore[a]	*Singapore*	87	Ibadan	*Nigeria*
74	Damascus[a]	*Syria*			

COMMODITIES AND MANUFACTURED GOODS.

Most countries use the Standard International Trade Classification (SITC) to describe the goods they import and trade. The classifications are periodically revised: SITC (3) was introduced in January 1988. A list of the main items follows.

There are 9 sections, giving single digits 1–9; divisions within these sections have 2-digit numbers, and groups within each division have 3-digit numbers. In the list below all sections and divisions are shown together with selected groups. There are also 4-digit subgroups in the SITC list, with, for example, 072.3 for "cocoa paste" as a subgroup of 072 ("cocoa"), and further breakdowns for some items into a 5-digit level, with, for example, 072.32 for "cocoa paste, wholly or partly defatted".

Throughout, nes stands for "not elsewhere specified".

0	Food and live animals
00	Live animals other than animals of division 03
01	Meat and meat preparations
02	Dairy products and birds' eggs
022	Milk and cream and milk products other than butter or cheese
023	Butter and other fats and oils derived from milk
024	Cheese and curd
03	Fish (not marine mammals), crustaceans, molluscs and aquatic invertebrates, and preparations thereof
04	Cereal and cereal production
041	Wheat (including spelt) and meslin, unmilled
042	Rice
043	Barley, unmilled
044	Maize (not including sweetcorn), unmilled
05	Vegetables and fruit

06   Sugar, sugar preparations and honey
07   Coffee, tea, cocoa, spices, and manufactures thereof
071   Coffee and coffee substitutes
072   Cocoa
074   Tea and maté
08   Feeding stuff for animals (not including unmilled cereals)
09   Miscellaneous edible products and preparations

1   Beverages and tobacco
11   Beverages
112   Alcoholic beverages
12   Tobacco and tobacco manufactures

2   Crude materials, inedible, except fuels
21   Hides, skins and furskins, raw
22   Oil seeds and oleaginous fruit
23   Crude rubber (including synthetic and reclaimed)
24   Cork and wood
25   Pulp and waste paper
26   Textile fibres (other than wool tops), and their wastes (not
      manufactured into yarn or fabric)
263   Cotton
266   Synthetic fibres suitable for spinning
267   Other man-made fibres suitable for spinning and waste of
      man-made fibres
268   Wool and other animal hair (including wool tops)
27   Crude fertilisers other than those of division 56 and crude
      minerals (excluding coal, petroleum and precious stones)
28   Metalliferous ores and metal scrap
281   Iron ore and concentrates
29   Crude animal and vegetable materials, nes

3   Mineral fuels, lubricants and related materials
32   Coal, coke and briquettes
33   Petroleum, petroleum products, and related materials
333   Petroleum oils and oils obtained from bituminous materials,
      crude
34   Gas, natural and manufactured
35   Electric current

4   Animal and vegetable oils, fats and waxes
41   Animal oils and fats
42   Fixed vegetable fats and oils; crude, refined or fractioned
43   Animal and vegetable oils and fats, processed and waxes of
      animal or vegetable origin; inedible mixtures or preparations
      of animal or vegetable fats and oils, nes
5   Chemical and related products, nes

51	Organic chemicals
52	Inorganic chemicals
53	Dyeing, tanning and colouring materials
54	Medicinal and pharmaceutical products
55	Essential oils, resinoids and perfume materials; toilet, polishing and cleansing preparations
56	Fertilisers (other than those of group 27)
57	Plastics in primary forms
58	Plastics in non-primary forms
59	Chemical materials and products, nes

6	Manufactured goods, classified chiefly by material
61	Leather, leather manufactures, nes and dressed furskins
62	Rubber manufactures, nes
63	Cork and wood manufactures (excluding furniture)
64	Paper, paperboard and articles of paper pulp, of paper or of paperboard
65	Textile yarn, fabrics, made-up articles, nes and related products
66	Non-metallic mineral manufactures, nes
67	Iron and steel
68	Non-ferrous metals
681	Silver, platinum and other metals of the platinum group
682	Copper
683	Nickel
684	Aluminium
687	Tin
69	Manufactures of metal, nes

7	Machinery and transport equipment
71	Power generating machinery and equipment
713	Internal combustion piston engines, and parts thereof, nes
72	Machinery specialised for particular industries
721	Agricultural machinery (excluding tractors) and parts thereof
724	Textile and leather machinery, and parts thereof, nes
73	Metalworking machinery
74	General industrial machinery and equipment, nes, and machine parts, nes
75	Office machines and automatic data processing machines
76	Telecommunications, sound recording and reproducing apparatus and equipment
761	Television receivers (including monitors and projectors) whether or not incorporating radio receivers or recording/reproducing apparatus
77	Electrical machinery, apparatus and appliances, nes and electrical parts thereof (including non-electrical counterparts, nes, of electrical household-type equipment)

78	Road vehicles (including air cushion vehicles)
781	Motor cars and other motor vehicles principally designed for the transport of persons (other than public transport vehicles
782	Motor vehicles for the transport of goods and special purpose motor vehicles
79	Other transport equipment
791	Railway vehicles (including hovertrains) and associated equipment
792	Aircraft and associated equipment; spacecraft (including satellites) and spacecraft launch vehicles
793	Ships, boats (including hovercraft) and floating structures
8	Miscellaneous manufactured articles
81	Prefabricated buildings; sanitary, plumbing, heating and lighting fixtures and fittings, nes
82	Furniture and parts thereof; bedding, mattresses, supports, cushions and similar stuffed furnishings
83	Travel goods, handbags and similar containers
84	Articles of apparel and clothing accessories
85	Footwear
87	Professional, scientific and controlling instruments and apparatus, nes
88	Photographic apparatus, equipment and supplies and optical goods, nes; watches and clocks
881	Photographic apparatus and equipment, nes
885	Watches and clocks
89	Miscellaneous manufactured articles, nes
9	Commodities and transactions not classified elsewhere in the SITC
911	Postal packages not classified according to kind
931	Special transactions and commodities not classified according to kind
961	Coin (other than gold coin) not being legal tender
981	Military arms and ammunitions

CURRENCIES.

Country	Currency	Symbol[a]
Afghanistan	afghani	Af
Albania	lek	Lk
Algeria	Algerian dinar	AD
Angola	kwanza	Kz
Argentina	austral	A
Australia	Australian dollar	A$
Austria	schilling	Sch
Bahamas	Bahamian dollar	B$
Bahrain	Bahrain dinar	BD
Bangladesh	taka	Tk
Barbados	Barbadian dollar	Bd$
Belgium	Belgian franc	BFr
Belize	Belizean dollar	Bz$
Benin	CFA franc	CFAfr
Bermuda	Bermuda dollar	Bda$
Bhutan	ngultrum	Nu
Bolivia	Boliviano	Bol
Botswana	pula	P
Brazil	cruzeiro	Cr
Brunei	Brunei dollar	Br$
Bulgaria	lev	Lv
Burkina Faso	CFA franc	CFAfr
Burundi	Burundi franc	Bufr
Cambodia	riel	CR
Cameroon	CFA franc	CFAfr
Canada	Canadian dollar	C$
Cape Verde	Cape Verde escudo	CVEsc
Central African Republic	CFA franc	CFAfr
Chad	CFA franc	CFAfr
Chile	Chilean peso	peso
China	yuan	Y
Colombia	Colombian peso	peso
Comoros	Comoran franc	Cfr
Congo	CFA franc	CFAfr
Costa Rica	Costa Rican colón	¢
Côte d'Ivoire	CFA franc	CFAfr
Cuba	Cuban peso	peso
Cyprus	Cyprus pound	C£
Czechoslovakia	koruna	Kcs
Denmark	Danish krone	DKr
Djibouti	Djibouti franc	Dfr
Dominican Republic	Dominican Republic peso	peso

Country	Currency	Symbol[a]
Ecuador	sucre	Su
Egypt	Egyptian pound	£E
El Salvador	El Salvador colón	¢
Equatorial Guinea	CFA franc	CFAfr
Ethiopia	birr	Birr
Fiji	Fiji dollar	F$
Finland	markka	Fmk
France	franc	Fr
Gabon	CFA franc	CFAfr
The Gambia	dalasi	D
Germany[b]	Deutschemark	DM
Ghana	cedi	C
Greece	drachma	Dr
Guatemala	quetzal	Q
Guinea	Guinean franc	Gfr
Guinea Bissau	Guinea Bissau peso	P
Guyana	Guyanese dollar	G$
Haiti	gourde	gourdes
Honduras	lempira	La
Hong Kong	Hong Kong dollar	HK$
Hungary	forint	Ft
Iceland	Iceland new króna	Ikr
India	Indian rupee	Rs
Indonesia	rupiah	Rp
Iran	rial	IR
Iraq	Iraqi dinar	ID
Ireland	Irish pound (punt)	I£
Israel	new shekel	NIS
Italy	lira (pl. lire)	L
Jamaica	Jamaican dollar	J$
Japan	yen	¥
Jordan	Jordan dinar	JD
Kenya	Kenya shilling	KSh
North Korea	won	Won
South Korea	won	W
Kuwait	Kuwaiti dinar	KD
Laos	kip	K
Lebanon	Lebanese pound	L£
Lesotho	loti (pl. maloti)	M
Liberia	Liberian dollar	L$
Libya	Libyan dinar	LD
Luxembourg	Luxembourg franc	Lfr
Macau	pataca	MPtc
Madagascar	Madagascar franc	Mgfr

Country	Currency	Symbol[a]
Malawi	kwacha	MK
Malaysia	Malaysian dollar/ringgit	M$
Mali	CFA franc	CFAfr
Malta	Maltese lira	Lm
Mauritania	ouguiya	UM
Mauritius	Mauritius rupee	MRs
Mexico	Mexican peso	peso
Morocco	dirham	Dh
Mozambique	metical	MT
Myanmar	kyat	Kt
Namibia	South African rand	R
Nepal	Nepalese rupee	NRs
Netherlands	guilder	G
Netherlands Antilles	Netherlands Antilles guilder	NAG
New Zealand	New Zealand dollar	NZ$
Nicaragua	córdoba	C
Niger	CFA franc	CFAfr
Nigeria	naira	N
Norway	Norwegian krone	NKr
Oman	Omani rial	OR
Pakistan	Pakistan rupee	PRs
Panama	balboa	B
Papua New Guinea	Kina	Kina
Paraguay	guarani	G
Peru	inti	In
Philippines	Philippine peso	P
Poland	zloty	Zl
Portugal	escudo	Esc
Puerto Rico	US dollar	$
Qatar	Qatari riyal	QR
Romania	leu (pl. lei)	Lei
Rwanda	Rwandan franc	Rwfr
São Tomé & Príncipe	dobra	Db
Saudi Arabia	Saudi riyal	SR
Senegal	CFA franc	CFAfr
Seychelles	Seychelles rupee	SRs
Sierra Leone	leone	Le
Singapore	Singaporean dollar	S$
Solomon Islands	Solomon Island dollar	SI$
Somalia	Somali shilling	SoSh
South Africa	rand	R
Soviet Union	rouble	Rb
Spain	peseta	Pta
Sri Lanka	Sri Lanka rupee	SLRs

Country	Currency	Symbol[a]
Sudan	Sudanese pound	S£
Suriname	Suriname guilder	SG
Swaziland	lilangeni (pl. emalengeni)	E
Sweden	Swedish krona	SKr
Switzerland	Swiss franc	SFr
Syria	Syrian pound	S£
Taiwan	New Taiwanese dollar	NT$
Tanzania	Tanzanian shilling	TSh
Thailand	baht	Bt
Togo	CFA franc	CFAfr
Tonga	Tonga dollar	T$
Trinidad & Tobago	Trinidad & Tobago dollar	TT$
Tunisia	Tunisian dinar	TD
Turkey	Turkish lira	TL
Uganda	New Ugandan shilling	NUSh
United Arab Emirates	UAE dirham	Dh
United Kingdom	pound/sterling	£
United States of America	dollar	$
Uruguay	Uruguayan new peso	peso
Vanuatu	vatu	Vt
Venezuela	bolívar	Bs
Vietnam	dong	D
Western Samoa	Tala	Tala
Windward & Leeward Isles[c]	East Caribbean dollar	EC$
North Yemen[d]	Yemeni rial	YR
South Yemen	Yemeni dinar	YD
Yugoslavia	Yugoslav dinar	YuD
Zaire	zaire	Z
Zambia	Zambian kwacha	ZK
Zimbabwe	Zimbabwe dollar	Z$

[a] These are the symbols formulated by the Economist Intelligence Unit and may be used in the text where a currency is often repeated. See also CURRENCIES (page 24) for *The Economist* newspaper usage.

[b] The East German mark (Ostmark, EM) was replaced by the Deutschemark in July 1990.

[c] Antigua & Barbuda, Dominica, Grenada, Monserrat, St Kitts-Nevis, St Lucia, St Vincent & Grenadines, the British Virgin islands.

[d] North and South Yemen merged to form the Yemen Republic in May 1990. The new joint currency is the Yemeni rial.

E

EARTHQUAKES. The Richter scale defines the magnitude of an earthquake in terms of the energy released.

Richter scale		Explosion equivalent	
	Joules	TNT *terms*	*Nuclear terms*
0[a]	7.9×10^2	175mg	
1	6.0×10^4	13g	
2	4.0×10^6	0.89kg	
3	2.4×10^8	53kg	
4	1.3×10^{10}	3 tons	
5[b]	6.3×10^{11}	140 tons	
6[c]	2.7×10^{13}	6 kilotons	$\frac{1}{3}$ atomic bomb
7	1.1×10^{15}	240 kilotons	12 atomic bombs
8	3.7×10^{16}	8.25 megatons	$\frac{1}{3}$ hydrogen bomb
9	1.1×10^{18}	250 megatons	13 hydrogen bombs
10	3.2×10^{19}	7,000 megatons	350 hydrogen bombs

[a] Approximately equal to the shock caused by an average man jumping from a table.

[b] Potentially damaging to structures.

[c] Potentially capable of general destruction; widespread damage is usually caused above magnitude 6.5.

Note: One atomic bomb is equivalent to 6.3 on the Richter scale, and one hydrogen bomb to 8.2.

Here are some examples.

	Richter scale
Mexico City, 1986	7.8
San Francisco, 1906	8.3
Chile, 1960	8.3
Krakatoa, 1883	9.9 (estimate)

ELEMENTS.

These are the natural and artificially created chemical elements.

Name	Symbol	Name	Symbol
Actinium	Ac	Iridium	Ir
Aluminium	Al	Iron (Ferrum)	Fe
Americium	Am	Krypton	Kr
Antimony (Stibium)	Sb	Lanthanum	La
Argon	Ar	Lawrencium	Lr
Arsenic	As	Lead (Plumbum)	Pb
Astatine	At	Lithium	Li
Barium	Ba	Lutetium	Lu
Berkelium	Bk	Magnesium	Mg
Beryllium	Be	Manganese	Mn
Bismuth	Bi	Mendelevium	Md
Boron	B	Mercury (Hydrargyrum)	Hg
Bromine	Br	Molybdenum	Mo
Cadmium	Cd	Neodymium	Nd
Caesium	Cs	Neon	Ne
Calcium	Ca	Neptunium	Np
Californium	Cf	Nickel	Ni
Carbon	C	Niobium	Nb
Cerium	Ce	Nitrogen	N
Chlorine	Cl	Nobelium	No
Chromium	Cr	Osmium	Os
Cobalt	Co	Oxygen	O
Copper (Cuprum)	Cu	Palladium	Pd
Curium	Cm	Phosphorus	P
Dysprosium	Dy	Platinum	Pt
Einsteinium	Es	Plutonium	Pu
Erbium	Er	Polonium	Po
Europium	Eu	Potassium (Kalium)	K
Fermium	Fm	Praseodymium	Pr
Fluorine	F	Promethium	Pm
Francium	Fr	Protactinium	Pa
Gadolinium	Gd	Radium	Ra
Gallium	Ga	Radon	Rn
Germanium	Ge	Rhenium	Re
Gold (Aurum)	Au	Rhodium	Rh
Hafnium	Hf	Rubidium	Rb
Hahnium	Ha	Ruthenium	Ru
Helium	He	Rutherfordium	Rf
Holmium	Ho	Samarium	Sm
Hydrogen	H	Scandium	Sc
Indium	In	Selenium	Se
Iodine	I	Silicon	Si

Name	Symbol	Name	Symbol
Silver (Argentum)	Ag	Tin (Stannum)	Sn
Sodium (Natrium)	Na	Titanium	Ti
Strontium	Sr	Tungsten (Wolfram)	W
Sulphur	S	Uranium	U
Tantalum	Ta	Vanadium	V
Technetium	Tc	Xenon	Xe
Tellurium	Te	Ytterbium	Yb
Terbium	Tb	Yttrium	Y
Thallium	Tl	Zinc	Zn
Thorium	Th	Zirconium	Zr
Thulium	Tm		

F

FRACTIONS. Do not mingle fractions with decimals. If you need to convert one to the other, use this table. See also FIGURES, page 29.

Fraction	Decimal equivalent
$1/2$	0.5
$1/3$	0.333
$1/4$	0.25
$1/5$	0.2
$1/6$	0.167
$1/7$	0.143
$1/8$	0.125
$1/9$	0.111
$1/10$	0.1
$1/11$	0.091
$1/12$	0.083
$1/13$	0.077
$1/14$	0.071
$1/15$	0.067
$1/16$	0.063
$1/17$	0.059
$1/18$	0.056
$1/19$	0.053
$1/20$	0.05

G

GEOLOGICAL ERAS. Astronomers and geologists give this broad outline of the ages of the universe and the earth.

Era, period and epoch		Years ago m	Characteristics
Origin of the universe		20,000	
(estimates vary		to	
markedly)		10,000	
Origin of the sun		5,000	
Origin of the earth		4,600	
Pre-Cambrian			
Archean		4,000	First signs of fossilised microbes
Proterozoic		2,500	
Palaeozoic			
Cambrian		570	First appearance of abundant fossils
Ordovician (obsolete)		500	Vertebrates emerge
Silurian		440	Fishes emerge
Devonian		400	Primitive plants emerge
Carboniferous		350	Amphibians emerge
Permian		270	Reptiles emerge
Mesozoic			
Triassic		250	Seed plants emerge
Jurassic		210	Age of dinosaurs
Cretaceous		145	Flowering plants emerge; dinosaurs extinct at end of this period
Cenozoic			
Palaeocene		65	
Tertiary:	Eocene	55	Mammals emerge
	Oligocene	40	
	Miocene	25	
	Pliocene	5	
Quaternary:	Pleistocene	2	Ice ages; stone age man emerges
	Holocene or Recent	10,000[a]	Modern man emerges

[a] 10,000 years, not 10,000m years.

L

LATIN.

Here are some common Latin words and phrases and their translations.

ab initio   from the beginning

ad hoc   for this object or purpose (implied and "this one only"); therefore, without a system, spontaneously

ad hominem   to an individual's interests or passions; used of an argument that takes advantage of the character of the person on the other side

ad infinitum   to infinity, that is, endlessly

ad lib. ad libitum, meaning at pleasure. Used adverbially or even as a verb when it means to invent or extemporise

ad valorem   according to value (as opposed to volume)

a fortiori   with stronger reason

annus mirabilis   wonderful year, used to describe a special year, one in which more than one memorable thing has happened; for instance 1666, the year of the Great Fire of London and the English defeats of the Dutch

a priori   from cause to effect, that is, deductively or from prior principle

cave   "Watch out!" (imperative); once used at boys' schools

caveat emptor   let the buyer beware

ceteris paribus   other things being equal

cf   short for *confer*, meaning compare

circa   around or about: used for dates and large quantities; can be abbreviated to *c* or *c.*

de facto   in point of fact

de jure   from the law; by right

de profundis   from the depths

deus ex machina   God from a machine; first used of a Greek theatrical convention, where a god would swing on to the stage, high up in a machine, solving humanly insoluble problems athus resolving the action of a play. Now used to describe a wholly outside person who puts matters right.

eg exempli gratia, for example

et al. et alii, and others, used as an abbreviation in bibliographies when citing multiple editorship or authorship to save the writer the bother of writing out all the names. Thus, A. Bloggs *et al., The Occurrence of Endangered Species in the Genus Orthodoptera*

ex cathedra   from the chair of office, authoritatively

ex officio   by virtue of one's office, not unofficially

ex parte   from or for one side only

ibid.   ibidem, in the same place; used in footnotes in academic works to mean that the quote comes from the same place, book, etc

idem   the same, that is mentioned before; like *ibidem*

ie   id est, that is, explains the material immediately in front of it

in absentia   in the absence of, used as "absent"

in camera   in a (private) room, that is, not in public

in re   in the matter of

in situ   in (its) original place

inter alia/inter alios   among other things or people

ipso facto   by that very fact, in the fact itself

loc. cit.   loco citato, in the place cited; used in footnotes to mean that the source of the reference or quote has already been given

mea culpa   my fault

mirabile dictu   literally, wonderful to relate

mutatis mutandis   after making the necessary changes

nem. con.   nemine contradicente, no one against; unanimously

op. cit.   opere citato, in the work quoted; similar to *loc. cit.* (q.v.)

pace   despite

pari passu   on the same terms, at an equal pace or rate of progress

passim   adverb, here and there or scattered. Used in indexes to indicate that the item is scattered throughout the work and there are too many instances to enumerate them all

persona non grata   person not in favour

petitio elenchis   the sin of assuming a conclusion

post eventum   after the event

post hoc, ergo, propter hoc   after this, therefore because of this. Used fallaciously in argument to show that because something comes after something it can be inferred that the first thing caused the second thing

post mortem   after death, used as an adjective and also as a noun, a clinical examination of a dead body

prima facie   at first sight, meaning apparently and having no connection with love

primus inter pares   first among equals

pro tem.   pro tempore, for the moment

PS   post scriptum, written afterwards

quid pro quo   something for something (or one thing for another), something in return, an equivalent; usually given

q.v.   quod vide, which see; means that the reader should look for the word just mentioned (eg in glossary)

re   with regard to, in the matter of

sic   thus; used in brackets in quotes to show writer has made a mistake. "Mrs Thacher (sic) resigned today."

sine die   without (setting) a date

status quo ante   the same state as before; shortened to *status quo*. A common usage is "maintaining the status quo"

stet   let it stand or do not delete; cancels an alteration in proof-reading; dots are placed under what is to remain

sub judice   under judgment or consideration; not yet decided

sub rosa   under the rose, privately or furtively; not the same as under the gooseberry bush

ultra vires   beyond (one's) legal power

vade mecum   a little book or something carried about on the person; literally "Go with me"

versus   shortened to *v* or *v.*, against; used in legal cases and games

Laws.

Scientific, economic, facetious and fatalistic laws in common use are listed here.

Boyle's Law. The pressure of a gas varies inversely with its volume at constant temperature.

Gresham's Law. When money of a high intrinsic value is in circulation with money of lesser value, it is the inferior currency which tends to remain in circulation, while the other is either hoarded or exported. In other words: "Bad money drives out good".

Grimm's Law. (Concerns mutations of the consonants in the various Germanic languages.) Proto-Indo-European voiced aspirated stops, voiced unaspirated stops and voiceless stops become respectively voiced unaspirated stops, voiceless stops and voiceless fricatives.

Heisenberg's Uncertainty Principle. Energy and time or position and momentum cannot both be accurately measured simultaneously. The product of their uncertainties is h (Planck's constant).

Hooke's Law. The stress imposed on a solid is directly proportional to the strain produced within the elastic limit.

Mendel's Principles. The Law of Segregation is that every somatic cell of an individual carries a pair of hereditary units for each character: the pairs separate during meiosis so that each gamete carries one unit only of each pair.

The Law of Independent Assortment is that the separation of units of each pair is not influenced by that of any other pair.

Murphy's Law. Anything that can go wrong will go wrong.

Ohm's Law. Electric current is directly proportional to electromotive force and inversely proportional to resistance.

Parkinson's Law. First published in *The Economist,* November 19th 1955. The author, C. Northcote Parkinson, sought to expand on the "commonplace observation that work expands so as to fill the time available for its completion". After studying Admiralty staffing levels, he concluded that in any public administrative department not actually at war the staff increase may be expected to follow this formula:

$$x = \frac{2k^m + p}{n}$$

Where k is the number of staff seeking promotion through the appointment of subordinates; p represents the difference between the ages of appointment and retirement; m is the number of hours devoted to answering minutes within the department; and n is the number of effective units being administered. Then x will be the number of new staff required each year.

Mathematicians will, of course, realise that to find the percentage increase they must multiply x by 100 and divide by the total of the previous year, thus:

$$\frac{100(2km + p)}{yn} \%$$

where y represents the total original staff. And this figure will invariably prove to be between 5.17% and 6.56%, irrespective of any variation in the amount of work (if any) to be done.

The Peter Principle. All members of a hierarchy rise to their own level of incompetence.

Say's Law of Markets. A supply of goods generates a demand for the goods.

Laws of Thermodynamics
1. The change in the internal energy of a system equals the sum of the heat added to the system and the work done on it.
2. Heat cannot be transferred from a colder to a hotter body within a system without net changes occurring in other bodies in the system.
3. It is impossible to reduce the temperature of a system to absolute zero in a finite number of steps.

Utz's Laws of Computer Programming. Any given program, when running, is obsolete. If a program is useful, it will have to be changed. Any given program will expand to fill all available memory.

Wolfe's Law of Journalism. You cannot hope/to bribe or twist,/ thank God! the/British journalist./But seeing what/the man will do/ unbribed, there's/no occasion to.

M

MEASURES

ROUGH CONVERSIONS. For British, American and metric (SI) measures. Metric units not generally recommended as SI units or for use with SI are marked with an asterisk (eg Calorie★).

Acceleration

Standard gravity	=	10 metres per second squared
	=	32 feet per second squared

Area

1 square inch	=	6½ square centimetres
2 square inches	=	13 square centimetres
10¾ square feet	=	1 square metre
43 square feet	=	4 square metres
6 square yards	=	5 square metres
2½ acres	=	1 hectare
5 acres	=	2 hectares
250 acres	=	1 square kilometre
3 square miles	=	8 square kilometres

Density and concentration

4 ounces per UK gallon	=	25 grams per litre
2 ounces per US gallon	=	15 grams per litre
1 pound per cubic foot	=	16 kilograms per cubic metre
62½ pounds per cubic foot	=	1 kilogram per litre
	=	density of 1

Energy

18 British thermal units	=	19 kilojoules
4 British thermal units	=	1 kilocalorie★
1 kilocalorie★ ("Calorie"★)	=	4 kilojoules

Force

7¼ poundals	=	1 newton
1 pound-force	=	4½ newtons
1 pounds-force	=	40 newtons
1 kilogram-force	=	10 newtons

Fuel consumption

5 UK gallons per mile	=	14 litres per kilometre
20 miles per UK gallon	=	7 kilometres per litre
20 miles per UK gallon	=	14 litres per 100 kilometres
5 miles per US gallon	=	6 miles per UK gallon

Length

Width of thumb	=	1 inch
	=	25 millimetres
1 inch	=	2½ centimetres
2 inches	=	5 centimetres
1 foot	=	30 centimetres
	=	0.3 metre
3¼ feet	=	1 metre
39 inches	=	1 metre
11 yards	=	10 metres
⅝ mile	=	1 kilometre
5 miles	=	8 kilometres
8 miles	=	7 nautical miles (international)

Power

4 UK horsepower	=	3 kilowatts
72 UK horsepower	=	73 metric horsepower★

Pressure and stress

1 pound-force per square foot	=	48 pascals (newtons per square metre)
1 pound-force per square inch	=	7 kilopascals (kilonewtons per square metre)
1 bar	=	1 standard atmosphere
	=	14½ pounds-force per square inch
100 pounds-force per square inch	=	7 kilograms-force per square centimetre

Velocity (speed)

2 miles per hour	=	3 feet per second
9 miles per hour	=	4 metres per second
8 kilometres per hour	=	5 metres per second
11 kilometres per hour	=	10 feet per second
30 miles per hour	=	48 kilometres per hour
50 miles per hour	=	80 kilometres per hour
70 miles per hour	=	113 kilometres per hou

Volume and capacity

1 teaspoonful	=	5 millilitres
1 UK fluid ounce	=	28 millilitres
26 UK fluid ounces	=	25 US liquid ounces
3 cubic inches	=	49 cubic centimetres
	=	49 millilitres
1¾ UK pints	=	1 litre
7 UK pints	=	4 litres
7 UK quarts	=	8 litres
5 UK pints	=	6 US liquid pints
9 US liquid pints	=	9 litres
1 UK gallon	=	4½ litres
2 UK gallons	=	9 litres

5 UK gallons	=	6 US gallons
1 US gallon	=	3³/₄ litres
4 US gallons	=	15 litres
3 cubic feet	=	85 cubic decimetres
	=	85 litres
35 cubic feet	=	1 cubic metre
4 cubic yards	=	3 cubic metres
31 UK bushels	=	32 US bushels
27¹/₂ UK bushels	=	1 cubic metre
28¹/₃ US bushels	=	1 cubic metre
11 UK bushels	=	4 hectolitres
14 US bushels	=	5 hectolitres
1 US bushel (heaped)	=	1¹/₄ US bushels (struck)
1 US dry barrel	=	3¹/₄ US bushels
1 US cranberry barrel	=	2³/₄ bushels
1 barrel (petroleum)	=	42 US gallons
	=	35 UK gallons
1 barrel per day	=	50 tonnes per year

Weight

1 grain	=	65 milligrams
15 grains	=	1 gram
11 ounces	=	10 ounces troy
1 ounce	=	28 grams
1 ounce troy	=	31 grams
1 pound	=	454 grams
5 ounces	=	1 kilogram
2¹/₄ pounds	=	1 kilogram
11 stones	=	70 kilograms
11 US hundredweights	=	5 quintals★
2 UK hundredweights	=	1 quintal★
2,205 pounds	=	1 tonne
11 US tons	=	10 tonnes
62 UK tons	=	63 tonnes
100 UK (long) tons	=	112 US (short) tons

Yield

3 UK or US bushels per acre	=	2 quintals★ per hectare
10 UK or US bushels per acre	=	9 hectolitres per hectare
1 UK hundredweight per acre	=	1¹/₄ quintals★ per hectare
1 UK ton per acre	=	2¹/₂ tonnes per hectare
9 pounds per acre	=	10 kilograms per hectare

METRIC SYSTEM PREFIXES.

Prefix name & symbol		Factor by which unit is multiplied	Description
atto	a	$10^{-18}=$ 0.000 000 000 000 000 001	
femto	f	$10^{-15}=$ 0.000 000 000 000 001	
pico	p	$10^{-12}=$ 0.000 000 000 001	million millionth; trillionth
nano	n	$10^{-9} =$ 0.000 000 001	thousand millionth; billionth
micro	μ	$10^{-6} =$ 0.000 001	millionth
milli	m	$10^{-3} =$ 0.001	thousandth
centi	c	$10^{-2} =$ 0.01	hundredth
deci	d	$10^{-1} =$ 0.1	tenth
deca (or deka)	da[a]	$10^{1} =$ 10	ten
hecto	h	$10^{2} =$ 100	hundred
kilo	k	$10^{3} =$ 1,000	thousand
myria	my	$10^{4} =$ 10,000	ten thousand
mega	M	$10^{6} =$ 1,000,000	million
giga	G	$10^{9} =$ 1,000,000,000	thousand million; billion
tera	T	$10^{12} =$ 1,000,000,000,000	million million; trillion
peta	P	$10^{15} =$ 1,000,000,000,000,000	
exa	E	$10^{18} =$ 1,000,000,000,000,000,000	

[a] Sometimes dk is used (eg in Germany).

UNITS WITH DIFFERENT EQUIVALENTS.
Barrel

UK (beer)	=	36 UK gallons
	=	164 litres
USA: dry standard	=	7,056 cubic inches
	=	116 litres
petroleum	=	42 US gallons
	=	159 litres
standard cranberry	=	5,826 cubic inches
	=	95.5 litres
various (liquid)	=	31–42 US gallons
	=	117–151 litres

Bushel

UK	=	2,219.36 cubic inches
	=	36.37 litres
Old English, Winchester⎫		
USA[a] (struck[b]) ⎭	=	2,150 42 cubic inches
	=	35.24 litres
USA (heaped)	=	2,747 715 cubic inches
	=	45.03 litres

[a] The most usual unit.
[b] Levelled off at the top.
[c] Used for apples.

Centner or Zentner

UK	=	cental of 100 pounds
	=	45.36 kilograms
Commercial hundredweight in several European countries, generally 50 kilograms	=	110.23 pounds
Metric centner of 100 kilograms	=	220.46 pounds

Chain

UK: Gunter's/surveyors'	=	66 feet
	=	20.12 metres}
Engineers'	=	100 feet
	=	30.48 metres

Foot

UK⎫		
USA customary ⎭	=	12 inches
	=	0.304 8 metre
USA survey	=	12.000 02 inches
	=	0.304 800 6 metre
Canada: Paris foot	=	12.789 inches
	=	0.325 metre
Cape foot	=	12.396 inches
	=	0.315 metre
Chinese foot (*che* or *chih*):		
old system	=	14.1 inches
	=	0.358 metre
new system	=	13.123 inches
	=	0.333 33 metre

Gallon

UK	=	277.42 cubic inches
	=	4.546 litres
Old English, Winchester, Wine⎫		
USA, liquid ⎭	=	231 cubic inches
	=	3.785 litres
USA, dry	=	268.802 5 cubic inches
	=	0.004 4 cubic metre

Gill

UK	=	8.669 cubic inches
	=	142.1 millilitres
USA	=	7.218 75 cubic inches
	=	118.3 millilitres

Hundredweight

UK ⎱ USA, long ⎰	=	112 pounds
	=	50.8 kilograms
USA, short	=	100 pounds
	=	45.4 kilograms

Link

UK: Gunter's/surveyors'	=	0.66 foot
	=	0.201 2 metre
Engineers'	=	1 foot
	=	0.304 8 metre

Mile

UK: imperial	=	5,280 feet
	=	1.609 344 kilometres
geographical ⎱ nautical ⎰ sea	=	6,080 feet
	=	1.853 184 kilometres[a]
USA	=	5,280 feet
	=	1.609 344 kilometres
International nautical	=	1,852 metres
	=	6,076.12 feet

[a] In practice sometimes 6,000 feet = 1.8288 kilometres

Ounce

Dry: ounce	=	437½ grains
	=	28.35 grams
ounce troy	=	480 grains
	=	31.01 grams
Liquid or fluid ounce: UK	=	1.734 cubic inches
	=	28.4 millilitres
USA	=	1.805 cubic inches
	=	29.6 millilitres

[a] 20 fluid ounces = 1 pint
[b] 16 liquid ounces = 1 liquid pint

Peck

UK	=	554.839 cubic inches
	=	9.092 cubic decimetres (litres)
USA	=	537.605 cubic inches
	=	8.810 cubic decimetres (litres)

Pint

UK	=	34.677 4 cubic inches
	=	0.568 litre

USA: dry =	33.600 312 5 cubic inches
=	0.551 cubic decimetre (litre)
liquid =	28.875 cubic inches
=	0.473 litre

Pound

UK ⎫	
USA ⎭ avoirdupois pound =	0.454 kilogram
USA: troy pound =	0.373 kilogram
=	0.823 pound (avoirdupois)
Spanish (libra) =	0.460 kilogram
=	1.014 pounds (avoirdupois)
"Amsterdam" =	0.494 kilogram
=	1.089 pounds (avoirdupois)
Danish (pund) =	0.5 kilogram
=	1.102 pounds (avoirdupois)
Française (livre) =	0.490 kilogram
=	1.079 pounds (avoirdupois)

Quart

UK =	69.355 cubic inches
=	1.137 litres
USA: dry =	67.200 625 cubic inches
=	1.101 cubic decimetres (litres)
liquid =	57.75 cubic inches
=	0.946 litre

Quarter

UK: capacity =	8 bushels
=	64 gallons
=	2.909 hectolitres
=	0.290 9 cubic metre
weight (mass) =	28 pounds
=	12.701 kilograms
cloth =	9 inches
=	22.86 centimetres
wines and spirits =	27½–30 gallons
=	125–136 litres

Quintal

Hundredweight: UK =	112 pounds
=	50.8 kilograms
USA =	100 pounds
=	45.4 kilograms
Metric quintal =	100 kilograms
=	220.46 pounds
Spanish quintal =	46 kilograms
=	101.4 pounds

Stone

UK: Imperial =	14 pounds
=	6.350 kilograms

Smithfield	=	8 pounds
	=	3.629 kilograms

Ton

UK: weight (mass)	=	2,240 pounds
	=	1.016 tonnes
shipping: register	=	100 cubic feet
	=	2.832 cubic metres
USA: short	=	2,000 pounds
	=	0.907 tonne
long	=	2,240 pounds
	=	1.016 tonnes
Metric ton (tonne)	=	1,000 kilograms
	=	2,204.62 pounds
Spanish:short (corta)	=	2,000 libras
	=	0.920 2 tonne
	=	2,028.7 pounds
long (larga)	=	2,240 libras
	=	1.030 6 tonnes
	=	2,272.1 pounds

See also MEASUREMENTS, page 41.

N

NATIONAL ACCOUNTS.
These are the definitions adopted by the United Nations in 1968.

Final expenditure
- = private final consumption expenditure ("consumers' expenditure")
- + government final consumption expenditure
- + increase in stocks
- + gross fixed capital formation
- + exports of goods and services

Gross domestic product (GDP) at market prices
- = final expenditure
- - imports of goods and services

Gross national product (GNP) at market prices
- = gross domestic product at market prices
- + net property income from other countries

Gross domestic product at factor cost
- = gross domestic product at market prices
- - indirect taxes
- + subsidies

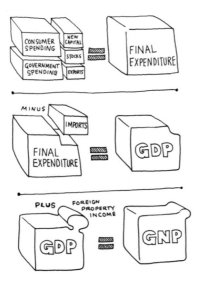

O

OLYMPIC GAMES.

I	Athens	1896	XIII	London (cancelled)	1944
II	Paris	1900	XIV	London	1948
III	St Louis	1904	XV	Helsinki	1952
	Athens	1906	XVI	Melbourne	1956
IV	London	1908	XVII	Rome	1960
V	Stockholm	1912	XVIII	Tokyo	1964
VI	Berlin (cancelled)	1916	XIX	Mexico City	1968
VII	Antwerp	1920	XX	Munich	1972
VIII	Paris	1924	XXI	Montreal	1976
IX	Amsterdam	1928	XXII	Moscow	1980
X	Los Angeles	1932	XXIII	Los Angeles	1984
XI	Berlin	1936	XXIV	Seoul	1988
XII	Tokyo/Helsinki	1940	XXV	Barcelona	1992
	(cancelled)		XXVI	Atlanta	1996

ORGANISATIONS

These are the exact names and abbreviated titles of the main international organisations. Where membership is small or exclusive, members are listed too.

ALADI. Latin American Integration Association.
Members

Argentina	Colombia[a]	Peru[a]
Bolivia[a]	Ecuador[a]	Uruguay
Brazil	Mexico	Venezuela[a]
Chile	Paraguay	

[a] These countries are also members of the Andean Group.

ASEAN. Association of South East Asian Nations.
Members

Brunei	Malaysia	Singapore
Indonesia	Philippines	Thailand

BIS. Bank for International Settlements. The central bankers' central bank, in Basle.

Members

Australia	Greece	Romania
Austria	Hungary	South Africa
Belgium	Iceland	Spain
Bulgaria	Ireland	Sweden
Canada	Italy	Switzerland
Czechoslovakia	Japan	Turkey
Denmark	Netherlands	United Kingdom
Finland	Norway	United States of
France	Poland	America
Germany	Portugal	Yugoslavia

CARICOM. Caribbean Community and Common Market.

Members

Antigua and Barbuda	Jamaica
Bahamas	Montserrat
Barbados	St Kitts-Nevis
Belize	St Lucia
Dominica	St Vincent and the Grenadines
Grenada	Trinidad and Tobago
Guyana	

COMECON. The Council for Mutual Economic Assistance, which was the communist world's version of the European Economic Community (see EC); dissolved.

Members

Bulgaria	Hungary	Romania
Czechoslovakia	Mongolia	Soviet Union
Cuba	Poland	Vietnam
East Germany		

COMMONWEALTH.

Members

Antigua and Barbuda	Ghana	Namibia
	Grenada	Nauru[a]
Australia	Guyana	New Zealand
Bahamas	India	Nigeria
Bangladesh	Jamaica	Pakistan[b]
Barbados	Kenya	Papua New Guinea
Belize	Kiribati	Seychelles
Botswana	Lesotho	Sierra Leone
Brunei	Malawi	Singapore
Canada	Malaysia	Solomon Islands
Cyprus	Maldives	Sri Lanka
Dominica	Malta	St Kitts-Nevis
	Mauritius	St Lucia

125

St Vincent and the	Tonga	United Kingdom
Grenadines	Trinidad and	Vanuatu
Swaziland	Tobago	Western Samoa
Tanzania	Tuvalu[a]	Zambia
The Gambia	Uganda	Zimbabwe

[a] Does not attend Commonwealth summits.
[b] Pakistan withdrew in 1972, but rejoined in 1989. Ireland and South Africa withdrew in 1949 and 1961 respectively. Fiji's membership lapsed in 1987 after the proclamation of a republic.

Dependencies and associated states
Australia:

Ashmore and Cartier Islands	Coral Sea Islands Territory
Australian Antarctic Territory	Heard and McDonald Islands
Christmas Island	Norfolk Island
Cocos (Keeling) Islands	

New Zealand:

Cook Islands	Ross Dependency
Niue	Tokelau

United Kingdom:

Anguilla	Gibraltar
Bermuda	Hong Kong (until 1997)
British Antarctic Territory	Isle of Man
British Indian Ocean Territory	Montserrat
British Virgin Islands	Pitcairn Islands
Cayman Islands	St Helena and dependencies
Channel Islands	Ascension
Falkland Islands and dependencies	Tristan da Cunha
South Georgia	Turks and Caicos Islands
South Sandwich Islands	

CSCE. Conference on Security and Co-operation in Europe. Originally founded in 1975. 34 members.

EC. European Community, the collective designation of three organisations with common membership. These organisations are: the European Coal and Steel Community (ECSC), European Economic Community (EEC) and European Atomic Energy Community (EURATOM). Their executives, which merged in 1967, are: the Commission of the European Communities, Council of Ministers of the European Communities, European Parliament, Court of Justice of the European Communities, Court of Auditors of

the European Communities and European Investment Bank.
Members

Belgium[a]	Greece	Netherlands[a]
Denmark	Ireland	Portugal
France[a]	Italy[a]	Spain
Germany[a]	Luxembourg[a]	United Kingdom

[a] Founding members.

ECOWAS. Economic Community of West African States.
Members

Benin	Guinea	Niger
Burkina Faso	Guinea-Bissau	Nigeria
Cape Verde	Liberia	Senegal
Côte d'Ivoire	Mali	Sierra Leone
The Gambia	Mauritania	Togo
Ghana		

EFTA. European Free Trade Association.
Members.

Austria	Iceland	Sweden
Finland	Norway	Switzerland

FRANC ZONE. Comité Monétaire de la Zone Franc.
Members

Benin[a]	Equatorial Guinea[b]
Burkina Faso[a]	France[c]
Cameroon[b]	Gabon[b]
Central African Republic[b]	Mali[a]
Chad[b]	Nigera
Comoros[b]	Senegal[a]
Congo[b]	Togo[a]
Côte d'Ivoire[a]	

[a] Member of Banque Centrale des Etats de l'Afrique de l'Ouest.
[b] Member of Banque des Etats de l'Afrique Centrale.
[c] Metropolitan France, Mayotte, St Pierre and Miquelon and the Overseas Departments and Territories.

GCC. Co-operation Council for the Arab States of the Gulf. Its normal shorthand name is Gulf Co-operation Council.
Members

Bahrain	Qatar
Kuwait	Saudi Arabia
Oman	United Arab Emirates

GROUP OF SEVEN (G-7). A subset of the G-10, whose members are Canada, France, Germany, Italy, Japan, UK and the USA. It has no organisational structure. Holds formal summit meetings of heads of state or their representatives. Although primarily a forum for discussing economic problems, the G-7 is increasingly becoming involved in politics.

GROUP OF TEN (G-10). The ten countries – the United States of America, the United Kingdom, Germany, France, Belgium, Netherlands, Italy, Sweden, Canada and Japan and an honorary eleventh member, Switzerland – that agreed to provide credit of $6 billion to the International Monetary Fund in 1962, known as the General Arrangement to Borrow. The G-10 is a convenient forum for discussing international monetary arrangements; it hatched the Smithsonian agreement and currency changes in 1971. The G-10 also meets through its central bank, the Bank for International Settlements (BIS) based in Basle.

IATA. International Air Transport Association. Head offices: Montreal and Geneva. *Members*: most international airlines.

NATO. North Atlantic Treaty Organisation.
Members

Belgium	Iceland	Portugal
Canada	Italy	Spain
Denmark	Luxembourg	Turkey
France[a]	Netherlands	United Kingdom
Germany	Norway	United States of America
Greece		

[a] France withdrew from the integrated military structure in 1966 but remains a member of the Atlantic Alliance.

OAU. Organization of African Unity.
Members

Algeria	Chad	Ghana
Angola	Comoros	Guinea
Benin	Congo	Guinea Bissau
Botswana	Côte d'Ivoire	Kenya
Burkina Faso	Djibouti	Lesotho
Burundi	Egypt	Liberia
Cameroon	Equatorial Guinea	Libya
Cape Verde	Ethiopia	Madagascar
Central African	Gabon	Malawi
Republic	The Gambia	Mali

Mauritania	Seychelles	Togo
Mauritius	Sierra Leone	Tunisia
Mozambique	Somalia	Uganda
Namibia	Sudan	Zaire
Niger	Swaziland	Zambia
Nigeria	São Tomé and	Zimbabwe
Rwanda	Príncipe	
Senegal	Tanzania	

The Sahara Arab Democratic Republic (Western Sahara) was admitted in February 1982, following recognition by 26 of the 50 members. Its membership was disputed by Morocco and others which claimed that a two-thirds majority was needed to admit a state whose existence is in question. Morocco withdrew from the OAU with effect from November 1985.

OAS. Organization of American States.
Members

Antigua and	Dominican	Peru
Barbuda	Republic	St Kitts-Nevis
Argentina	Ecuador	St Lucia
Bahamas	El Salvador	St Vincent and the
Barbados	Grenada	Grenadines
Bolivia	Guatemala	Suriname
Brazil	Haiti	Trinidad and
Canada	Honduras	Tobago
Chile	Jamaica	United States of
Colombia	Mexico	America
Costa Rica	Nicaragua	Uruguay
Cuba	Panama	Venezuela
Dominica	Paraguay	

OECD. Organisation for Economic Co-operation and Development. Capitalism's club, based in Paris.
Members

Australia	Greece	Norway
Austria	Iceland	Portugal
Belgium	Ireland	Spain
Canada	Italy	Sweden
Denmark	Japan	Switzerland
Finland	Luxembourg	Turkey
France	Netherlands	United Kingdom
Germany	New Zealand	United States of America

Yugoslavia has a special status, halfway between observer and partici-
pant.

OPEC. Organization of Petroleum Exporting Countries.
Members

Algeria	Iraq	Qatar
Ecuador	Kuwait	Saudi Arabia
Gabon	Libya	United Arab Emirates
Indonesia	Nigeria	Venezuela
Iran		

THE UNITED NATIONS. New York.
Main bodies

General Assembly	Trusteeship Council
Security Council	International Court of Justice
Economic and Social Council Secretariat (ECOSOC)	

Regional Commissions of ECOSOC		*Head office*
Economic Commission for Africa	ECA	Addis Ababa
Economic Commission for Europe	ECE	Geneva
Economic and Social Commission for Asia and the Pacific	ESCAP	Bangkok
Economic Commission for Latin America and the Caribbean	ECLAC	Santiago, Chile
Economic and Social Commission for Western Asia	ESCWA	Baghdad

Other United Nations bodies		
International Sea-Bed Authority		Kingston, Jamaica
Office of the United Nations Disaster Relief Co-ordinator	UNDRO	Geneva
United Nations Centre for Human Settlements	UNCHS (HABITAT)	Nairobi
United Nations Children's Fund	UNICEF[a]	New York
United Nations Conference on Trade and Development	UNCTAD	Geneva
United Nations Development Programme	UNDP	New York
United Nations Environment Programme	UNEP	Nairobi
United Nations High Commissioner for Refugees	UNHCR	Geneva
United Nations Observer Missions and Peace-keeping Forces		New York
United Nations Population Fund	UNFPA[b]	New York

United Nations Relief and Works Agency for Palestine Refugees in the Near East	UNRWA	Vienna
World Food Council	WFC	Rome
World Food Programme	WFP	Rome

[a] Formerly the United Nations Children's Emergency Fund.
[b] Formerly the United Nations Fund for Population Activities.

Specialised agencies within the UN system

Food and Agriculture Organization	FAO	Rome
General Agreement on Tariffs and Trade	GATT	Geneva
International Atomic Energy Agency	IAEA	Vienna
International Bank for Reconstruction and Development (World Bank)	IBRD	Washington, DC
International Civil Aviation Organization	ICAO	Montreal
International Development Association	IDA	Washington, DC
International Finance Corporation	IFC	Washington, DC
International Fund for Agricultural Development	IFAD	Rome
International Labour Organisation	ILO	Geneva
International Maritime Organization	IMO	London
International Monetary Fund	IMF	Washington, DC
International Telecommunications Union	ITU	Geneva
Multilateral Investment Guarantee Agency	MIGA	Washington, DC
United Nations Educational, Scientific and Cultural Organization	UNESCO	Paris
United Nations Industrial Development Organization	UNIDO	Vienna
Universal Postal Union	UPU	Berne
World Health Organization	WHO	Geneva
World Intellectual Property Organization	WIPO	Geneva
World Meteorological Organization	WMO	Geneva

WARSAW PACT. Warsaw Treaty of Friendship, Co-operation and Mutual Assistance, the communist world's defence pact; dissolved.

Members

Bulgaria	Hungary	Romania
Czechoslovakia	Poland	Soviet Union
East Germany		

R

ROMAN NUMERALS.

I	1	XIII	13	XC	90
II	2	XIV	14	C	100
III	3	XV	15	CC	200
IV	4	XVI	16	D	500
V	5	XVII	17	DCC	700
VI	6	XVIII	18	DCCXIX	719
VII	7	XIX	19	CM	900
VIII	8	XX	20	M	1000
IX	9	XXI	21	MC	1100
X	10	XXX	30	MCX	1110
XI	11	XL	40	MCMXCI	1991
XII	12	L	50	MM	2000

S

STATES, REGIONS, PROVINCES, COUNTIES

Here are the correct spellings of the main administrative subdivisions of industrialised countries. Accents should be used. See also COUNTRIES AND THEIR INHABITANTS.

AUSTRALIA (Commonwealth of Australia)

States
New South Wales
Queensland
South Australia
Tasmania
Victoria
Western Australia

Territories
Australian Capital Territory
Northern Territory

BELGIUM (Kingdom of Belgium)

Provinces
Antwerp (Anvers)
Brabant
East Flanders (Oost-Vlaanderen)
Hainaut
Liège

Limburg
Luxembourg
Namur
West Flanders
  (West-Vlaanderen)

BRAZIL (Federal Republic of Brazil)

States
Acre
Alagoas
Amapá
Amazonas
Bahia
Ceará
Espírito Santo
Goiás
Maranhão
Mato Grosso
Mato Grosso do Sul
Minas Gerais
Pará
Paraíba

Paraná
Pernambuco
Piauí
Rio de Janeiro
Rio Grande do Norte
Rio Grande do Sul
Rondônia
Roraima
Santa Catarina
São Paulo
Sergipe
Tocantins
Distrito Federal
  (Federal District, Brasília)

CANADA
Provinces

Alberta
British Columbia
Manitoba
New Brunswick
Newfoundland
Nova Scotia
Ontario

Prince Edward Island
Quebec (Québec)
Saskatchewan

Territories
Northwest Territories
Yukon Territory

FRANCE (Republic of France)
Regions

Alsace
Aquitaine
Auvergne
Basse Normandie
Brittany (Bretagne)
Burgundy (Bourgogne)
Centre
Champagne-Ardenne
Corsica (Corse)
Franche Comté
Haute Normandie

Ile-de-France
Languedoc-Roussillon
Limousin
Lorraine
Midi-Pyrénées
Nord Pas-de-Calais
Pays de la Loire
Picardy (Picardie)
Poitou-Charentes
Provence Alpes Côte d'Azur
Rhône-Alpes

GERMANY (Federal Republic of Germany)
States (in German *Länder*)

Berlin[a]
Baden-Württemberg
Bavaria (Bayern)
Brandenburg[b]
Bremen
Hamburg
Hesse (Hessen)
Lower Saxony (Niedersachsen)
Thuringia (Thüringen)[b]
Mecklenburg-Vorpommern[b]

North Rhine-Westphalia
   (Nordrhein-Westfalen)
Rhineland-Palatinate
   (Rheinland-Pfalz)
Saarland
Saxony (Sachsen)[b]
Saxony-Anhalt (Sachsen-
   Anhalt)[b]
Schleswig-Holstein

[a] Formerly West Berlin.
[b] Former East German states.

IRELAND (Republic of Ireland)

Provinces	*Counties*	
Connacht	Galway	Roscommon
	Leitrim	Sligo
	Mayo	
Leinster	Carlow	Louth
	Dublin	Meath
	Kildare	Offaly

	Kilkenny	Westmeath
	Laois	Wexford
	Longford	Wicklow
Munster	Clare	Limerick
	Cork	Tipperary
	Kerry	Waterford
Ulster	Cavan	Monaghan
	Donegal	

ITALY (Italian Republic)
Regions

Abruzzi
Basilicata
Calabria
Campania
Emilia-Romagna
Friuli-Venezia Giulia
Lazio
Liguria
Lombardy (Lombardia)
Marche

Molise
Piedmont (Piemonte)
Puglia
Sardinia (Sardegna)
Sicily (Sicilia)
Tuscany (Toscana)
Trentino-Alto Adige
Umbria
Valle d'Aosta
Veneto

NETHERLANDS (Kingdom of the Netherlands)
Provinces

Drente
Flevoland
Friesland
Gelderland
Groningen
Limburg

Noord Brabant
Noord Holland
Overijssel
Utrecht
Zeeland
Zuid-Holland

SOVIET UNION (Union of Soviet Socialist Republics)

The country that used to be called the **Soviet Union** is in turmoil, with some parts leaving to become independent countries and others changing their names. Indeed the name Soviet Union is itself no longer officially correct, though the alternative **Union of Sovereign States** has yet to catch on. Until stability is achieved, the names below will serve. It should be noted, however, that Estonia, Latvia and Lithuania may now be considered independent countries.

Soviet Socialist Republics (SSRs)

Armenian (Armenia)
Azerbaijan
Belorussian (Belorussia)
Georgian (Georgia)
Kazakh (Kazakhstan)
Kirgiz (Kirgizia)

Moldavian (Moldavia)
Russian SFSR (Russia)
Tajik (Tajikistan)
Turkmen ((Turkmenistan)
Ukrainian (Ukraine)
Uzbek (Uzbekistan)

Autonomous Soviet Socialist Republics (ASSRs)
Within RSFSR:

Bashkir	Mari
Buryat	Mordovian
Chechen-Ingush	North Ossetian
Chuvash	Tatar
Dagestan	Tuva
Kabardino-Balkar	Udmurt
Kalmyk	Yakut
Komi	

Within Azerbaijan: Nakhichevan
Within Georgia: Abkhazia, Adzhar
Within Uzbekistan: Karakalpak

Autonomous Regions
Within RSFSR: Adygei, Gorno-Altai, Jewish,
            Karachai-Cherkess, Khakass
Within Azerbaijan: Nagorno-Karabakh
Within Georgia: South Ossetian
Within Tajikistan: Gorno-Badakhshan

SPAIN

Autonomous Communities

Andalucía	Catalonia (Cataluña)
Aragón	Extremadura
Asturias	Galicia
Balearic Islands (Baleares)	Madrid
Basque Country (Euskadi)	Murcia
Canary Islands (Canarias)	Navarra
Cantabria	Rioja
Castilla Y León	Valencia
Castilla-La Mancha	

UNITED KINGDOM

England: *Counties*

Avon	Devon	Hertfordshire
Bedfordshire	Dorset	Humberside
Berkshire	Durham	Isle of Wight
Buckinghamshire	East Sussex	Kent
Cambridgeshire	Essex	Lancashire
Cheshire	Gloucestershire	Leicestershire
Cleveland	Greater London[a]	Lincolnshire
Cornwall/Isles of	Greater Manchester[a]	Merseyside[a]
Scilly	Hampshire	Norfolk
Cumbria	Hereford and	North Yorkshire
Derbyshire	Worcester	Northamptonshire

Northumberland
Nottinghamshire
Oxfordshire
Shropshire
Somerset
South Yorkshire[a]
Staffordshire
Suffolk
Surrey
Tyne & Wear[a]
Warwickshire
West Midlands[a]
West Sussex
West Yorkshire[a]
Wiltshire

[a] Created in 1974 when local government was reorganised. Their councils were abolished in 1986.

Wales: Counties

Clwyd
Dyfed
Gwent
Gwynedd
Mid Glamorgan
Powys
South Glamorgan
West Glamorgan

Scotland: Regions

Borders
Central
Dumfries and
  Galloway
Fife
Grampian
Highland
Lothian
Orkney
Shetland
Strathclyde
Tayside
Western Isles

Northern Ireland: Districts

Antrim
Ards
Armagh
Ballymena
Ballymoney
Banbridge
Belfast
Carrickfergus
Castlereagh
Coleraine
Cookstown
Craigavon
Down
Dungannon
Fermanagh
Larne
Limavady
Lisburn
Londonderry
Magherafelt
Moyle
Newry and Mourne
Newtownabbey
North Down
Omagh
Strabane

UNITED STATES OF AMERICA

States

Alabama
Alaska
Arizona
Arkansas
California
Colorado
Connecticut
Delaware
Federal District of
  Columbia (DC)
Florida
Georgia
Hawaii
Idaho
Illinois
Indiana
Iowa
Kansas
Kentucky
Louisiana
Maine
Maryland
Massachusetts
Michigan
Minnesota
Mississippi
Missouri
Montana
Nebraska
Nevada
New Hampshire
New Jersey
New Mexico
New York
North Carolina
North Dakota
Ohio
Oklahoma
Oregon
Pennsylvania
Rhode Island
South Carolina

South Dakota	Vermont	Wisconsin
Tennessee	Virginia	Wyoming
Texas	Washington	
Utah	West Viginia	

YUGOSLAVIA (Socialist Federal Republic of Yugoslavia)
Republics

Bosnia and Herzegovina	Montenegro (Crna Gora)
(Bosnia-Hercegovina)	Serbia (Srbija)
Croatia (Hrvatska)	Slovenia (Slovenija)
Macedonia (Makedonija)	

Autonomous Provinces
Within Serbia: Vojvodina, Kosovo

STOCK MARKET INDICES.
January 1991. These lists are frequently changed. Most of these COMPANIES are public limited companies (PLCs).

THE FINANCIAL TIMES ORDINARY SHARE INDEX (the 30 Share Index) consists of the following.

Allied-Lyons	GKN
ASDA Group	Guinness
BICC	Hanson
BOC Group (The)	Hawker Siddeley Group
BTR	Lucas Industries
Blue Circle Industries	Imperial Chemical Industries
Boots Co. (The)	National Westminster Bank
British Airways	Marks and Spencer
British Gas	Peninsular & Oriental Steam
British Petroleum Company (The)	Navigation Co. (The)
British Telecommunications	Royal Insurance Holdings
Cadbury Schweppes	SmithKline Beecham
Courtaulds	Tate & Lyle
General Electric Company (The)	Thorn EMI
Glaxo Holdings	Trusthouse Forte
Grand Metropolitan	

THE FINANCIAL TIMES STOCK EXCHANGE 100 SHARE INDEX consists of the following.

Abbey National	BAA
Allied-Lyons	B.A.T Industries
Anglian Water	BET
Argyll Group	BICC
ASDA Group	BOC Group (The)
Associated British Foods	BTR

Bank of Scotland
(The Governor & Company of the)
Barclays
Bass
Blue Circle Industries
Boots Co. (The)
BPB Industries
British Aerospace
British Airways
British Gas
British Petroleum Company (The)
British Steel
British Telecommunications
Burmah Castrol
Cable and Wireless
Cadbury Schweppes
Commercial Union Assurance Co.
Courtaulds
Dalgety
Enterprise Oil
Eurotunnel
Fisons
GKN
General Accident Fire and Life Assurance Corporation
General Electric Company (The)
Glaxo Holdings
Grand Metropolitan
Great Universal Stores (The)
Guardian Royal Exchange
Guinness
Hammerson Property Investment and Development Corporation (The)
Hanson
Harrisons & Crosfield
Hawker Siddeley Group
Hillsdown Holdings
Imperial Chemical Industries
Kingfisher
LASMO
Ladbroke Group
Land Securities

Legal & General Group
Lloyds Bank
Lonrho
Lucas Industries
MEPC
Marks and Spencer
Maxwell Communication Corp.
Midland Bank
National Westminster Bank
North West Water Group
Peninsular & Oriental Steam Navigation Company (The)
Pearson
Pilkington
Prudential Corporation
RMC Group
RTZ Corporation (The)
Racal Electronics
Rank Organisation (The)
Ranks Hovis McDougall
Reckitt & Colman
Redland
Reed International
Reuters Holdings
Rolls-Royce
Rothmans International
Royal Bank of Scotland (The)
Royal Insurance Holdings
STC
Sainsbury (J)
Scottish & Newcastle Breweries
Sears
Severn Trent
'Shell' Transport and Trading Co
Smith & Nephew
SmithKline Beecham
Sun Alliance Group
TSB Group
Tarmac
Tesco
Thames Water
Thorn EMI
Trafalgar House
Trusthouse Forte
Ultramar

Unilever
United Biscuits (Holdings)
Wellcome

Whitbread & Company
Wiggins Group
Willis Corroon

THE DOW JONES INDUSTRIAL AVERAGE consists of the following companies.

Allied-Signal
Aluminum Co. of America (ALCOA)
American Express Co.
American Telephone & Telegraph Co.
Bethlehem Steel Corp.
Boeing Company (The)
Chevron Corp.
Coca-Cola Co. (The)
E.I. Du Pont de Nemours & Co.
Eastman Kodak Co.
Exxon Corp.
General Electric Co.
General Motors Corp.
Goodyear Tire & Rubber Company (The)
International Business Machines Corp.
International Paper Co.
McDonald's Corp.
Merck & Co.
Minnesota Mining & Manufacturing Co.
Navistar International Corp.
Philip Morris Cos.
Primerica Corp.
Procter & Gamble Co.
Sears Roebuck & Co.
Texaco
USX Corp.
Union Carbide Corp.
United Technologies Corp.
Westinghouse Electric Corp.
F.W. Woolworth Co.

Y

YACHTING. Here is a list of national sail letters of some of the countries which are members of the International Yacht Racing Union.
There will be new codes for the 1992 Olympics.

A	Argentina	L	Finland
B	Belgium	M	Hungary
BL	Brazil	MO	Monaco
BU	Bulgaria	N	Norway
CY	Sri Lanka	OE	Austria
CZ	Czechoslovakia	P	Portugal
D	Denmark	PH	Philippines
E	Spain	PZ	Poland
F	France	RC	Cuba
G	Germany	RI	Indonesia
GR	Greece	RM	Romania
H	Netherlands	S	Sweden
I	Italy	SA	South Africa
J	Japan	SR	Soviet Union
K	United Kingdom	TK	Turkey
KA	Australia	U	Uruguay
KB	Bermuda	US	United States of America
KC	Canada	V	Venezuela
KK	Kenya	X	Chile
KS	Singapore	Y	Yugoslavia
KZ	New Zealand	Z	Switzerland

INDEX